about the

author

Naomi Findlay

Naomi Findlay is the CEO of Silk Home and the Principal and Founder of the International Institute of Home Staging, author of the best-selling book Ignite Your Property Mojo, and the founder of NaomiFindlay.com.

Naomi specialises in teaching people how to sell their home for more, renovate for profit, or start a home staging business in an emerging and growing sector, and is known for using presale property styling to achieve sales prices more than $50,000 above expected figures using small investments of just a few thousand dollars.

Naomi produces and speaks at the Australian Home Staging Symposium each year, and has also presented at the American National Home Staging Summit.

She is a regular contributor to realestate.com.au, and is also a featured industry expert on RenoAddict.com.

Naomi has been featured as a contributing author or a guest expert in various media, including Home Beautiful, Smart Property Investment, Australian Property Investor Magazine, News.com, The Daily Telegraph, Newcastle Morning Herald Newspaper, Interiors Addict, She knows, Women's Agenda, Dear September, and Sold Digital Blogs.

Naomi has received teaching excellence awards from the University of Newcastle and the Australian College of Education, and been nominated for a national award with the Australian Teaching and Learning Council.

An authority among industry leaders, Naomi has mentored other experts in the field, including design business owners Alisa and Lysandra Fraser after their first appearance on "The Block" on the Nine Network, as well as other noteworthy personalities in the field of home staging and real estate.

THE TAILORED INTERIO

LOUIS VUITTON ARCHITECTURE

foreword

Never has renovating for profit been more popular, while when selling your own home, usually your biggest asset, you'd be crazy not to try and get the best price for it. Naomi Findlay combines years of experience at flipping her own investment properties, running a successful home staging business and educating other people in how to do the same through her International Institute of Home Staging.

As the cliche goes, what she doesn't know about selling your property for more isn't worth knowing! Naomi is generous with her knowledge and imparts it in a no-nonsense, easy to follow way, thanks to her years as a university lecturer. Her own business success story, and her passion for helping everyone get the best price for their property, is infectious and inspiring. Congratulations on a wise book purchase!

Jen Bishop
Publisher
Interiors Addict and Reno Addict

introduction

Do you want to sell your property for more, increase your rental yield, maximise your valuation to expand your borrowings or leverage your equity?

Then let me show you how

I have been buying and selling property for more than 15 years, and each time I sell, rent or have the property valued, I leverage my position using just a few simple techniques.

Every day around the world, people are buying and selling property. It is one of the most valuable assets a person can own - and when it comes time for it to be sold, they can either make the most of what they've got to come out on top, or show little interest in maximising its saleability and so end up disappointed with the final sale price.

But just what are the defining points that determine the success of any real estate sale?

PLACE

Location can be everything when it comes to buying and selling property. As the saying goes, it's all about 'location, location, location...'

PRICE

The price is an instrumental factor in a successful transaction. A property that is too highly priced will never sell, while a property that is priced too low will obviously sell, but not with the maximum gain for the vendor/owner.

MARKETING

The way you deliver any product to the market has an impact on the eventual outcome. For example if you sold two equal and equivalent products but one was not marketed, described or launched at all, would the outcome of the sales of these products be equal? No!

The exact same concept can be and must be applied to your property. Its marketing must be a primary consideration as the best property will not sell well if it is not marketed and handled well. This is why the selection of an agent to market your property is critical.

PRESENTATION

The final key to the success of any property transaction is the way the product is packaged and presented to the market. Just look at the way this can affect the sale and price point of products sold in an everyday commercial setting such as a supermarket. You could have two different packets of sugar, one the supermarket's own no-name brand and the other a brand that is a household name. In essence, you've got the same raw product - sugar. But the way the commercial brand presents its product; the styling of the package, the quality of its finish, the advertising used to promote it, means that they can price it much higher than their plainly-packaged competitor, based on the first impression it makes on the consumer.

If we translate this to the sale of property, it is simple to see the impact and power property presentation can have on the outcome of its sale. You can read more about this later in this book.

Marketing

Place

SALE

Price

Presentation

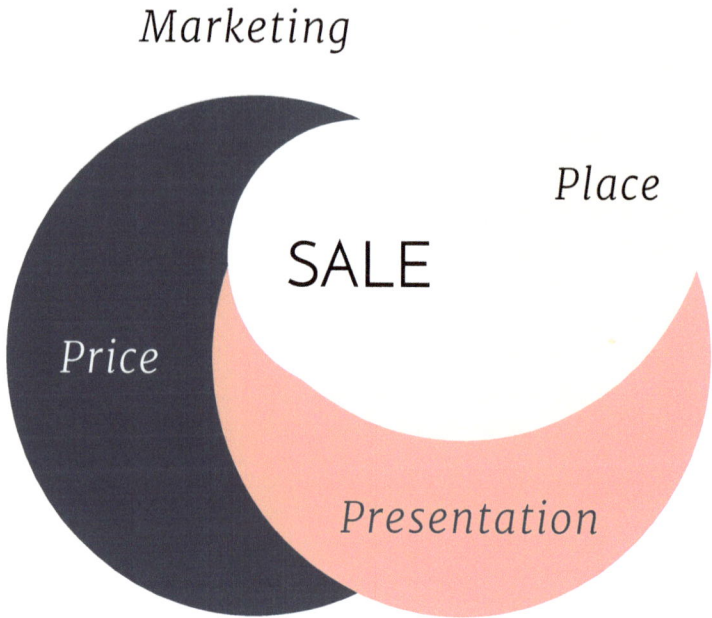

But if you look at the four key elements above, which are crucial in the successful sale of your property, you'll realise that you can exercise complete control over three of them.

Location is of course the sticking point. You already own the property, so there is little you can do about where it is situated, or how it relates to the developments, vistas and environment around it.

But you do have total control over the other three elements. And in this book you will learn the tried and tested methods I use when it comes to property presentation, which will help you maximise your sale price, increase your property value and use this leverage to get the most from your property and investments.

To start with let's consider the situation from a buyer's perspective...

Let's imagine it is Saturday and you have a long list of properties to inspect. You're looking for the ideal property for you and your family to buy or rent.

The first property you approach seems like a run-of-the-mill home. The lawns present okay but the house lacks street appeal. When you enter the property, you are hit by the overwhelming sense of other people's everyday clutter; there are shoes at the door, mail on the kitchen bench and dog food bowls on the back deck. Instead of being won over by the space on offer, you spend most of your time looking at the family photos on the walls and wondering where they purchased the bright, patterned bedspreads.

Many other properties you inspect after this one present in a similar manner. But amongst this sea of properties that seem to blend into one another, there is one property that stands out from the rest.

When you approach this property it seems to be well kept and well maintained. When you enter the home it is clutter-free and clean. The home is furnished in a simple, yet current style.

Walking through the home you find yourself thinking, "I can imagine sitting on that deck

"Home staging is a systematic process that involves many elements and aspects of maintenance, marketing and styling."

Naomi Findlay PhD

with friends ... our stuff would fit perfectly in here ... it's so well maintained there is nothing we would have to do unless we wanted to."

At the end of your day of inspections, the well-presented home is the property that stands out from the crowd. It's the one you want to go back and view for a second time.

Now imagine you are the seller of the wonderfully-presented property. In the lead-up to the first open home you made a small investment of time and money preparing the property to make a great first impression. You spent approximately $2000 engaging a professional home stager, hiring a few key accessories and renting some off-site storage. You attended to all small maintenance issues, de-cluttered and cleaned like you had never cleaned before. Your return on investment is a perfectly presented home that stood out from the competition and captured buyers' attention.

You have given your property the best chance of selling for the maximum sale price in the shortest time frame possible.

Although the personal situation of each property investor or owner can be very different, you all have one thing in common: you want to sell your home for the best possible price in the shortest possible time.

Focusing on the presentation of your property and presenting an exceptional product is a proven method to help you achieve this. The process of preparing a property for sale, valuation or rental is called home staging.

While home staging was not well known in Australia until recent years, it has been used successfully overseas for decades, helping vendors and owners achieve great results on the sale of their properties.

Through this book I will introduce you to the concept of home staging and pre-sale property styling, discuss its benefits and, most importantly, outline how the practices and principles of home staging will help you achieve your financial goals.

I will provide you with some tools to assist you in making sound decisions when staging your property.

And finally, I will reveal the eight key elements you must consider if you are preparing your property for sale or trying to increase the value of your property.

chapter 1

WHAT IS HOME STAGING?

What is home staging?

Home staging is an essential marketing tool when selling a property. It is the process of preparing your property for sale in a way that gives you the best chance of achieving the maximum sale price in the quickest possible time, by leveraging its presentation. Some people refer to home staging as 'house fluffing', which in the past gave the impression that preparing your house for sale was simply about the frills or finishing touches... or maybe about fluffing pillows!

THIS MISCONCEPTION IS FAR FROM THE TRUTH.

Home staging is a systematic process that involves many elements and aspects of maintenance, marketing and styling. All of these elements combine to provide a synergistic effect that showcases your property's strong points to make sure your property outshines its competition.

Put simply, home staging involves presenting your property at its best before the property goes to the market, to ensure it appeals to the widest possible range of buyers.

Many real estate experts comment on the importance of the first impression when selling your property, suggesting that the first 30 to 60 seconds is when many properties are sold.

Presenting your property in a way that makes the buyer say 'wow' as they drive up the street, 'wow' as they go through the front door and 'wow' as they enter the first room is extremely important to its sale.

What home staging and pre-sale property presentation is not...

IT IS NOT INTERIOR DESIGN OR INTERIOR DECORATING.

When I complete interior design work for a client, the project is all about them. The scope of the job encompasses the functionality, colour palette and styling tastes of the client and noone else. It is all about how the client wants to live and feel within their space.

In contrast, when I prepare a client's property for sale, the client or vendor is totally removed from the picture. The process of preparing your property for sale still uses solid design principles, but I combine these with my knowledge of the property market. I convert the property from one that tells a story about the owner or occupier into a marketable product aimed at the target audience.

Whilst there are multiple elements that make up the process of home staging, it is also important to clarify that home staging does not mean you have to empty your property of all the contents and fill it with expensive designer items and furnishings.

Some of these factors are out of your control, such as location and market conditions. But you do have total control over the condition and presentation of the property.

You can never be guaranteed a specific result when you put your property on the market. However, taking control of the condition and presentation of your property by using home staging principles ensures you have given yourself the best possible chance of achieving the highest possible sale price in the shortest possible time frame.

By taking control of this aspect of the property sale, you are making sure that you are not leaving money on the table for the buyer.

WHAT ARE THE BENEFITS OF HOME STAGING?

Market statistics have shown that a staged property will sell 30 to 50% faster than an equivalent un-staged property. Similarly it will sell for 7 to 17% more than its un-staged equivalent, with an average of 10% increase in sale price.

Research also tells us that many people are time poor and want to move into a property where there is "nothing to do". In fact, 83% of people will pay a premium price for a property that is presented well and needs no work done on it.

There are many factors that influence the sale of your property, including but not limited to:

- *market conditions;*
- *property condition;*
- *asking price;*
- *property presentation;*
- *marketing;*
- *the agents and their strategies; and*
- *location.*

Let's look at these numbers a bit more closely. If we were selling a $400,000 property, based on the above statistics you would sell your property for a minimum of $28,000 more, compared to not staging the property.

If you were selling a $700,000 property, the increase in sale price for staging the property would be in the vicinity of more than $49,000.

example 1

Vendor investment:
Professional staging consultation - $200
Accessory / furniture hire - $932

Selling price: $2,000,000
Investment in staging is
0.0005% of the sale price.

example 2

Vendor investment:
Professional staging consultation - $200
Accessory / furniture hire - $141

Selling price: $750,000
Investment in staging is
0.0003% of the sale price.

example 3

Vendor investment:
Professional staging consultation - $150
Accessory / furniture hire - $287

Selling price: $625,000
Investment in staging is 0.0006%
of the sale price.

Let's look at some real life examples of clever financial investments made by my recent clients...

It is important to realise that a financial benefit is gained not only as a result of maximising the sale price, but also by minimising the length of time you are paying loan or interest repayments on the property's finance whilst it is on the market.

There are many other benefits to staging your property for sale from a sorting, organising and pre-packing perspective, but these are mainly relevant to owner-occupiers, so I will not expand on them here.

However, as I alluded to in the introduction, home staging is not just for when you are selling your property. It is also a very successful tool to use when you are having a property valued for the purpose of unlocking some equity to help expand your property portfolio.

WHAT INVESTMENT DO YOU HAVE TO MAKE TO GET THESE BENEFITS?

There are two primary types of investment that you can make in staging your property:

- a time investment
- a financial investment
- a combination of both

WHY DOES HOME STAGING WORK?

Home staging works on many levels; below is an outline of the primary mechanisms:

1. Home staging makes your property stand out on the internet.

Research tells us that at least 80% of people shortlist and shop for property on the internet. Buyers prefer to save their valuable time by inspecting only properties that have caught their eye and met their criteria based on what they have seen on the internet listing. Staging your property will make sure the internet marketing images have the 'wow' factor that compels the buyer to shortlist your property.

2. Home staging helps to create the image of a lifestyle the property will offer the buyer.

This will engage and emotionally connect the buyer to the property. Creating engagement and emotional connection is an advantage in any stage of the property cycle, because once buyers have fallen in love with a property they will want to secure it before someone else beats them to it.

3. Only 5% of people are able to visualise what to do with a space and how to live in it.

This means that when viewing an empty property, 95% of people are left thinking, "That won't work for us, the rooms look so small," or, "I don't know what to do with this space."

Home staging helps people connect with spaces and shows them how the spaces can be used. At the same time, rooms look larger when furnished correctly. Home staging can also create rooms within rooms for open-planned spaces.

4. A staged property accentuates the beauty of a property – drawing attention to its highlights.

By selling a home's highlights, staging provides a "must-have" experience for potential buyers viewing a property. It creates an emotional connection with the buyers by portraying the idea they are buying a lifestyle - not just four walls.

5. People spend more time viewing staged homes.

Data from stagedhomes.com.au reveals that buyers spend 10 to 15 minutes longer viewing a property during the open inspection of a staged house, compared with that of an un-staged property.

6. A staged property projects the image of a well-maintained property.

The majority of buyers want to purchase a property with very little to do. A staged home that presents well, with little or no obvious maintenance or running repairs needed, projects the image of a well-maintained and cared for property. This image adds value to and increases the appeal of the property.

7. Good agents enjoy selling well-staged property.

Consider the agent's perspective; they are marketing a property that:

- will sell quicker, for a premium price;
- has good open home inspection attendance due to the attractive online presence;
- is a high quality, well-presented product.

This results in you having a motivated agent, who is excited about selling your property, working with you to achieve a great outcome.

8. A good home stager will work with your real estate agent to identify your target market.

They will then stage the home accordingly and market your property to that spectrum of buyers. This ensures that when the buyers inspect the property they emotionally connect with it and imagine themselves living in the space. A well staged property allows the buyers to imagine their furniture and possessions in the space and visualise themselves living there.

9. Bringing the buyers together.

Some of you may be reading this and thinking that you can see beyond all the clutter or beyond the fancy styling and that you only look at the 'bones' of the home. And in fact, you more than likely can.

However, not everyone is like you!

Without overwhelming you with physiology, when you are marketing a property it is important to understand the way humans think.

The brain is, broadly speaking, divided in two halves. Most of us think and act using predominantly one side of the brain, either our left or right brain. Very few of us are masters of whole brain thinking.

The characteristics of a left or right-brained thinker are vastly different. The table below describes the almost opposing characteristics of left versus right-brain thinkers.

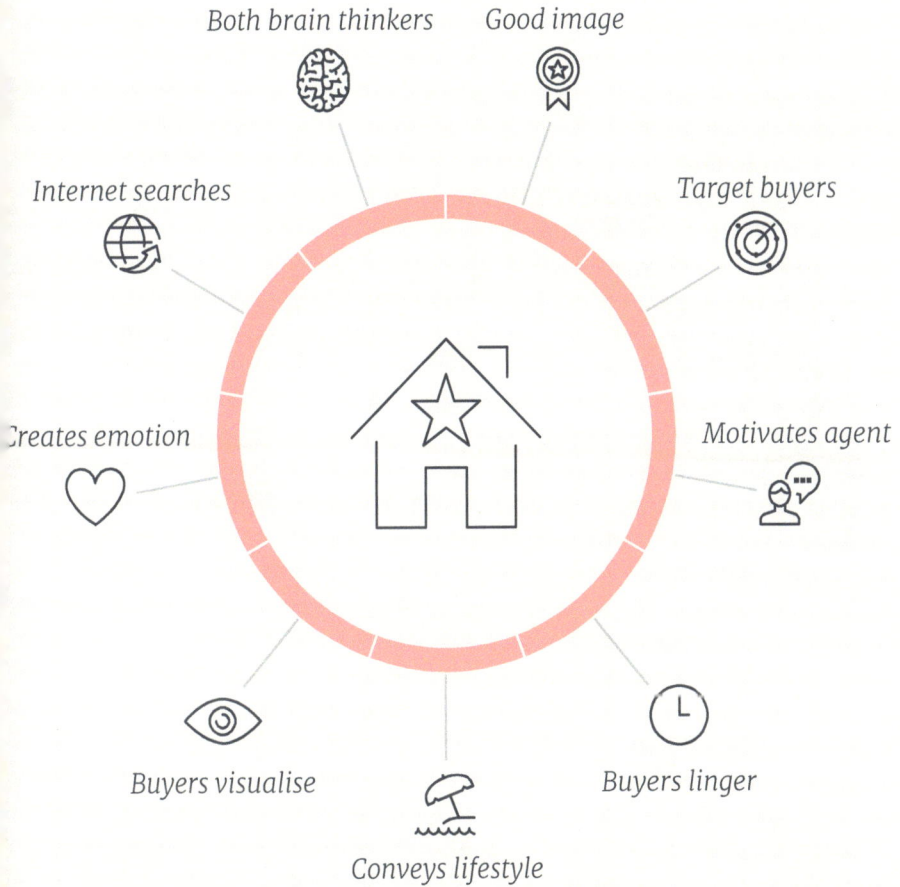

Both brain thinkers

Good image

Internet searches

Target buyers

Creates emotion

Motivates agent

Buyers visualise

Buyers linger

Conveys lifestyle

There is some evidence or discussion in literature on the theory that many couples, close friends or business partners often complement each other, one being a right-brained thinker and the other a left-brained thinker.

When staging a property you must make sure that the property appeals to both.

Characteristics of a left brain thinker	Characteristics of a right brain thinker
Logical	Random
Sequential	Intuitive
Rational	Holistic
Analytical	Emotive
Objective	Subjective
Looks at parts	Looks at things in whole

WHEN SHOULD YOU CONSIDER HOME STAGING?

Home staging is also about adding value to your property – but there's more than one reason you might want to increase the value of your property.

While the obvious motivation is that you are putting your house on the market, increasing the value of your property can also be useful when it comes to rental yield, or for a valuation when you are looking to unlock some equity.

STAGING A PROPERTY FOR RENT

Like staging a property to sell, it's important to consider your target market. Is it a three-bedroom house with two living areas and a large back yard close to schools? If so, present the home in a way that will appeal to a young family.

Or is it an inner city two-bed unit in a funky complex? In that case it's important to choose sleeker, more contemporary pieces to appeal to a young professional couple.

Many landlords may be wary of spending money on staging their rental property because of the possible high turnover of tenants.

"Will I have to stage every 12 months as tenants move out?"

Consider investing in staging just once and have it done professionally by an expert. Then hire a professional photographer to come in and snap shots of the property while it looks amazing. These shots can be used down the track when seeking new tenants, either on the real estate agent's website or in a posh-looking display book on the kitchen bench of the property.

If staging yourself, don't forget to use neutral colours and keep it simple, neat and clean looking. The message you are trying to convey is that this is an easy, no fuss rental.

You want potential renters to leave the property thinking that the landlord must be great if the property is in such good condition and the current tenant will clearly leave it in great shape.

Staging your rental property is essential in new, large complexes where there are multiple units being offered for rent and the monthly rental is negotiable.

Potential tenants will pay more for your property if it looks warm and welcoming as opposed to the un-staged unit next door that felt lifeless and cold.

If you're wanting to keep costs down, consider only staging key areas of the property. This would most likely be the living area, master bedroom, kitchen/dining (bar stools and minimal accessories on bench tops). Ensure the entry is warm and inviting as first impressions are key.

When you should use home staging

1. Checklist @ end of Chapter 9 - mechanisms of home staging checklist
2. Calculation of ROI via link www.naomifindlay.com/ bookbonus download on excel calculation sheet

Before you get started, you need to take three very important steps:

1. Let go of your old home.
2. Work out what help you need.
3. Set a budget and stick to it.

HOME STAGING STATISTICS

When investing in the presentation of a property for sale, owners and agents want to know their investment is worthwhile. Here are some Australian Home Staging Statistics...

LESS THAN 1%

Average investment in home staging was between 0.4-0.75% of estimated property value.

15% MORE

A staged property yields an average increase in sale price of 10% with a maximum increase reported of 15%.

20-FOLD RETURN ON INVESTMENT

On average, for every $1 invested in property staging, the property owner received a return of $20.

chapter 2

STARTING OUT ON YOUR HOME STAGING JOURNEY

"Selling your home is expensive. But more often than not, putting money into your property to make it more appealing to potential buyers can really pay off – literally!"

Naomi Findlay PhD

1. Letting go

Moving home can be extremely distressing, as can settling into your new abode, so ease the transition by saying a proper goodbye. This means more than forwarding your mail and registering with your new council, but rather focusing on the memories. Here's how to go about it:

Get snap happy

Documenting your old house before you've packed up all your stuff not only captures your home in its true state but will also give you a snapshot of your life in that exact moment. If you have kids, make sure you capture them in the photos too, so that when you're all older you can look back together fondly.

It's party time

Invite your closest friends and family and host a goodbye party. Don't worry about the moving boxes or the mess; just have some music playing, some paper plates and a BBQ.

Be a tourist

When you've lived somewhere for a long time you often avoid the official tours and local tourist traps. But now, with departure on the horizon, visit all the major destinations and see how your city/town presents itself compared to how you've come to know it. Who knows, you may even learn something knew.

2. The three groups of people you NEED when selling your home

When you look at a well staged home, what you may not know is that there were an array of people behind it! There's the elbow grease gang, the professional experts and the selling staff.

All three teams of people are absolutely vital and without all of them working together, getting that high bid come sale day may not be possible.

So who's who and why do you need them all?

Well first there's the elbow grease gang, which as the name suggests are the people who get in and get things done! They are most commonly the property owners, their friends and family and in some cases, hired labour. Their jobs include decluttering, cleaning, organising, packing, gardening and small repairs.

The professional experts come next and include professional home stagers, building inspectors, handymen, landscape gardeners, movers and tradies. It's these people, along with the elbow grease gang, that get the home looking in tip top shape.

When it comes to engaging the experts, the process below will help you identify who you need to help you and what things you can do on your own.

Firstly, think about the time you have available to dedicate to preparing your property for sale.

Next, work out the finances you have available and are willing to spend on the process.

The answers to these two questions will help you determine how much of the process you can complete yourself, as well as how much help you are going to need – and whether you can afford it!

Now take a look at the tasks that need to be completed. Divide the tasks into the following categories:

- General maintenance.
- Property repair or updating.
- Decluttering.
- Cleaning.
- Styling and Display.

For each item, first determine if you are qualified to do the task and then consider whether you will do as good a job as a professional.

For each task you indicate you can complete yourself, write next to it any cost (eg materials) involved and the time you will need to complete the task.

If you have opted to outsource the task, indicate the approximate cost of doing so.

Once you have worked out where and how you want to allocate your time and financial resources, take the lists to the relevant trades.

A professional home stager can assist you at any stage of the process, from helping identify the work that needs to be done, to being consulted for guidance on the final styling and presentation of the property.

But really, the people doing the hands-on work to stage your property are only part of the equation. After all, if no one's marketing a property, even the best dressed home will go for less than it's worth. This is where the selling staff come in - so picking the right team is crucial!

Some questions to consider when selecting your selling staff are:

- Are they personable?
- Are they honest?
- Do they have great communication skills?
- Do they know your property like the back of their hand?
- Do they have an excellent sales track record?

These are some great questions and tips to use when on the hunt for the perfect team, but make sure more than anything, that you trust your gut. After all no one knows your property the way you do. So get help, but make sure you do your research and trust your intuition!

"Don't be afraid of spending some money early on in the selling process. Time and time again it's been shown that staging your home is essential for securing the biggest profit come sale day."

Naomi Findlay PhD

3. How to pick a budget and stick to it!

Selling your home is expensive. But more often than not, putting money into your property to make it more appealing to potential buyers can really pay off - literally!

Of course, the question is, how much do you spend on home staging and making your property sale-day ready? What's too much and what's too little?

Well, first things first, you need to do your research. It is so vital that in the lead-up to selling you home you research other properties that are on the market and are your direct competition. From there you can figure out how much you can or should allocate to preparing your home for sale, and divide up your resources according to what needs to be completed.

From a financial perspective it is essential to ensure every dollar being invested into your home is worth it.

A rule of thumb is for every dollar you invest you should see at least $4 back in your pocket, giving you a 400% return on investment.

It sounds massive, but believe me it is achievable! The best way to work this out is to compare the sale price of a staged home against that of an equivalent un-staged home. From there you work backwards to obtain what the maximum investment should be for staging your home.

But what do you do if there are no recent sales of equivalent staged and un-staged homes in your area? You have two options; Google and an expert real estate agent! A good agent should know the worth of having a home staged and they should also be able to put you in contact with a professional home stager to determine the potential increase in property value.

Don't be afraid of spending some money early on in the selling process. Time and time again it's been shown that staging your home is essential for securing the biggest profit come sale day

Head over to book bonus page for ROI calculator

www.naomifindlay.com/bookbonus

chapter 3

DECLUTTERING YOUR PROPERTY

"It is a well-known fact that decluttering is an important step and an effective strategy to help you make more money when you sell your property."

Naomi Findlay PhD

Clutter can be frustrating, overwhelming and stressful, impacting on your ability to deal with day-to-day situations in the way you might like to.

Research has proven the link between the clarity of a person's mental state and the amount of visual clutter in their home. Case studies have shown that clutter leads to poor time management because it causes distraction and hinders us from finding what we need quickly.

In many cases it is also associated with depression and stress because of the overstimulating effect it has and the anxiety we create about dealing with it.

As a professional home styler, I know that a clean and organised living space is key to maintaining a positive state of mind and promoting positive emotional health for the entire family.

But it is also a well-known fact that decluttering is an important step and an effective strategy to help you make more money when you sell your property.

To some people this is a simple and streamlined activity that might be only a small part of the home staging process. However for others this is an epic and onerous task that for many and varied reasons can seem insurmountable.

In this chapter I will help you get started, and most importantly, complete the process of decluttering your property for sale.

I will guide you through the process of decluttering your drawers, cupboards, benches or the whole house – but the key to long-term success is developing new habits.

Room — What room are you working on?	What was the item?	What did your little voice tell you?

Task	Room	Component	Who	Resource, Checklist Completed?

So let's get started...

WHAT IS HOLDING YOU BACK?

Do you find yourself saying any of the following?

- I know where everything is, even though it is a mess!
- If I put it away I will lose it!
- I can't throw that out, what if I need it at some stage?
- I hate throwing things away!
- I can't throw that away because it has sentimental value!
- I know I don't wear it or use it BUT it was so expensive I can't possibly throw it away.
- I know it doesn't fit me now, but it will when I lose 10 kilos.

If you have said yes to any of these, you are perfectly normal. Many people I work with believe more than just one of these is true for them.

This is the root of what is really holding you back - and this is where mindset is important.

Mindset is the key to most things in life. In this chapter we are going to focus on the pragmatic side of decluttering and taking action.

SO TO START...

Be kind to yourself. There is no need to beat yourself up about how and why you have managed to accumulate so much clutter. Most of us have busy lives and do our best to stay on top of things. Instead of using time and energy giving yourself a hard time about it, simply shake it off and focus on what you ARE going to do about it.

A good exercise is to move from room to room and take note of some of the "limiting thoughts" or "voices" in your head as you tell yourself why you should keep things.

Making a choice and changing the way you think about de-cluttering can be the key; a clear and focused mindset can mean that de-cluttering is no longer a chore, it is an achievement and takes you one step closer to selling your property for more.

THE DECLUTTER DASH!

Clutter control is 100% achievable and a simple way to get on top of it is with the Declutter Dash.

When you have finished one Dash, repeat for every room and challenge yourself to decrease the number of items you choose to keep second time round.

One way to sustain clutter control is to take 'before' and 'after' photos to remind yourself not to undo the hard work you have just put in.

Before you attempt your first Declutter Dash, it is important to have a plan that includes:

- Who is going to do it? Identify your team. If you can't find any volunteers, that's not unusual - fortunately this is a job you can tackle on your own if you have to.

- What resources will you need? Bin bags and storage boxes could be helpful. This will become clear as we move through the chapter (see the resources checklist).

- Which rooms will take priority? Identify the rooms that are irking you the most, then outline the key components in each room that need to be addressed.

- When can you do this? Set a target date for each of the tasks to be completed. I recommend breaking it up into small chunks throughout the day or the weekend as setting aside a whole weekend for this process can be overwhelming and physically draining.

The Declutter Dash
RULES

Below are the rules of a Declutter Dash: they have been designed to be realistic, manageable and most of all, satisfying.

1. The "dash" takes no longer than 15 minutes.

2. You may not tackle a whole room per "dash". Select only one component of a room and do it thoroughly rather than addressing a bigger space that cannot be done in 15 minutes.

3. Once you pick up an item, you may not put it down. Make an instant decision about what to do with it - it must be sorted accordingly.

4. Once you have made your decision, you cannot change your mind, you must go onto the next thing.

5. Reward yourself at the end of each Dash. Have a cup of tea, watch an episode of your favourite show or read a chapter of a book. You've earned it!

RESOURCES CHECKLIST:

Marker pens	
Boxes	
Masking tape	
Cleaning products	

THE DECLUTTERING PROCESS

Step 1

Let's start by looking at your lifestyle, your home and what areas of the home impact on you the most in relation to the visual clutter.

- Is it your bedroom? Does it prevent you from getting a good night's sleep?
- Is it the kitchen drawers? Are they in such a mess you can never find anything?
- Is it your home office or study nook? Does it make you feel like the day-to-day running of the home is overwhelming?
- Is it the laundry? Does it make you feel as though it is a never-ending task that is even more insurmountable than it really is?
- Or your living space? Is your living space so cluttered you feel you do not have the space to escape and relax.

Have a good think about it and make a list. This will help you identify those areas of the house that are your best "bang for buck" and where to start first on your spring declutter efforts.

The sooner you see results the more motivated you will be to do more and more!

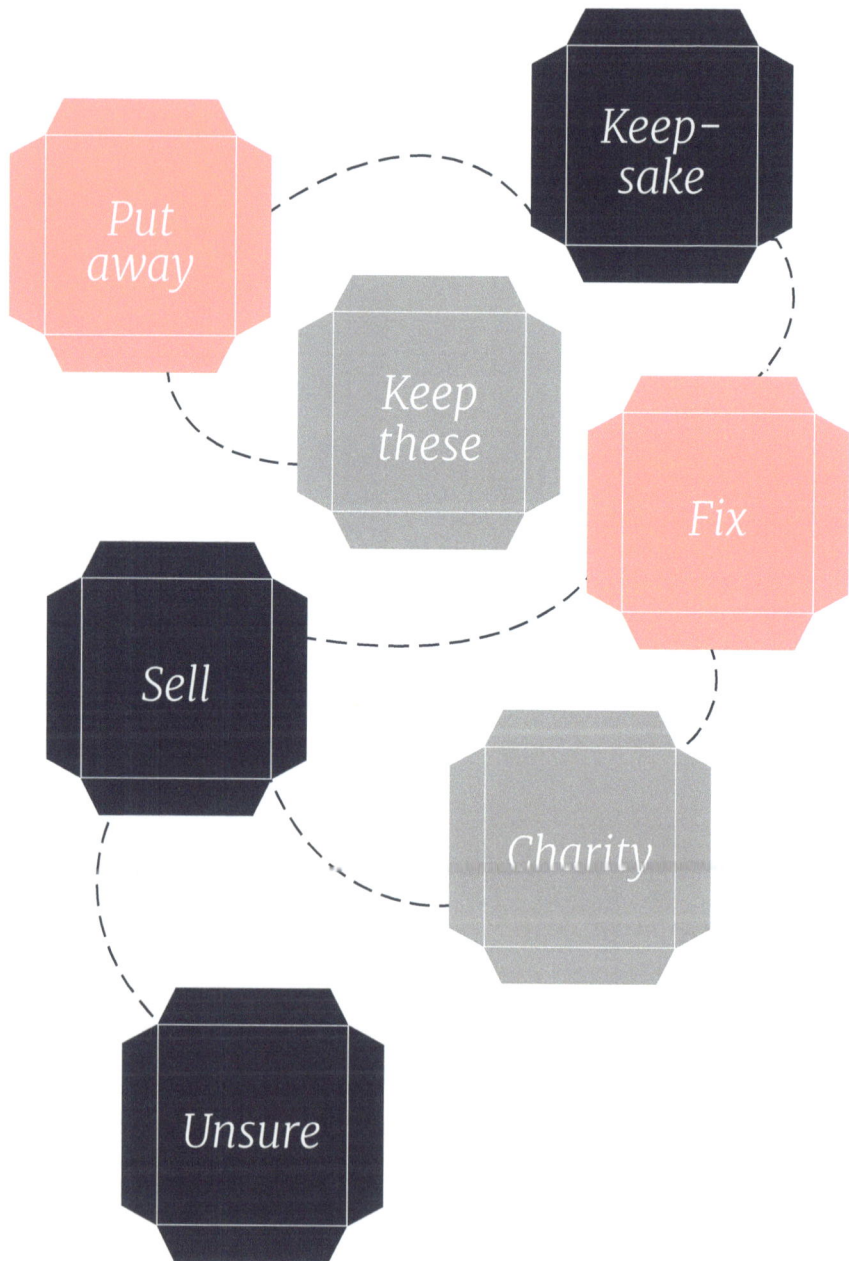

Put away

Keep-sake

Keep these

Fix

Sell

Charity

Unsure

Step 2

You need to get yourself some boxes or bags and label them as follows:

Put away - this is for the things that belong in this space. To keep them in the room you need to find a place for them to live within that room. This is not a case of "I want to keep this, I will find a spot for it later". This is about saying "I want to keep this and HERE is a spot for it to live".

Keep these - items you want to keep but they do not belong in this space. These items must go into the box and once you have finished the space take them to a space where you think they should remain. This does not mean on top of a cabinet or in the junk drawer, you must find a permanent and appropriate home for the item. If you are unable to do so they need to go into the unsure box for now!

Unsure - this box needs to be filled with items.

Sell - things that you are interested in selling as they might give you some extra cash.

Charity - items in good working order that you do not think are worthwhile selling, don't have time to sell or you would prefer to give to someone less fortunate than yourself.

Fix - anything that is broken or of ill repair goes in this box! The box then goes into the garage and lives there until you fix the items. Items can be removed if you fix them.

Keepsake - this box is for items you use rarely (once every five years) but have decided it is essential you keep.

Item	Function	Room used for	Elsewhere used	Room to store it

Step 3

Empty the space! Look at your action plan and follow it to the letter - that way there are no excuses! If you have chosen your bedroom as the first place to start, pick off one component of that room to begin.

Let's say it is the bedside table. You need to empty the bedside table! It is very important that you don't bite off more than you can chew in one chunk or you may find that you create more clutter and grief for yourself than you had to begin with. Remember the Declutter Dash!

Step 4

Use a staging area. It's also important that you set aside some space to do your sorting, somewhere that is open and central, maybe even the dining table. This way you won't be tempted to leave the items out to get back to later. You will be more motivated to get it done and get it done fast so you can return the open space to normal.

Step 5

Challenge yourself! Once you have chosen your space, emptied it and filled up the table or staging area you are ready to start again! That's right, once is not enough! Set yourself the challenge to reduce the items on the table even further in the second round of the Declutter Dash.

Step 6

Clean! There is no better time to clean than when a space is empty! This is your chance to give all your shelves and drawers a quick wipe over whilst they are empty, to save doubling up on work.

To make this job even easier have a packet of baby cleansing wipes beside you; they are user-friendly and gentle enough to use on most surfaces. The best part is they are low on nasty chemicals and hence your hands do not end up looking like prunes at the end of the day, nor do you have to wear gloves.

Step 7

Finishing off the job properly. You have come so far and achieved so much - let's make it count and have some longevity! Do it once, do it right and you will be set up for success!

When working out where and how to put things back in the space you have just decluttered, I want you to utilise the concept of zoning.

Zoning is the placing of items for a particular task where they are needed and will be used. This means you are NOT always placing like and like together.

Zoning then increases the chances of you replacing the item where it belongs once you have finished with it, without having to use a lot of effort or thought.

WHY DOES THIS WORK?
IT'S A LAW OF PHYSICS

The path of least resistance. In physics, the path of least resistance is always taken by objects moving through a system. For example, water flowing downhill follows the path of least resistance as it is pulled downward by gravity.

As humans we are no exception to the rule; in most cases when faced with a task we will choose the path of least resistance and hence the path that takes us the least effort and time.

Zoning items in our home essentially provides the path of least resistance all the time and GREATLY increases our chances of returning an item to where it belongs - thus avoiding the trap of it becoming clutter.

Let's consider an example: Think about where your toothbrush routinely lives. Do you find yourself constantly finding it around all different areas of the house and having to take it back to where it "lives"? Every client I have ever worked with replies 'NO' to this question. Why is this? This is because in 99% of cases the toothbrush is stored right next to where it is used, and hence putting it away is not an effort or a bother.

Let's imagine that you decided to store your toothbrush beside your bed rather than in the bathroom. I guarantee that you will regularly find your toothbrush in the bathroom and have to return it to the place you have chosen to store it, because you have NOT zoned the toothbrush correctly.

To help you determine the correct location for many of your items I have created a "function and zone" list of questions below. Use these for every item you are replacing and make sure it is zoned correctly for its function!

Step 8

Sensible storage! There is no doubt that having ample storage in a home can help minimise the clutter that can accumulate. However, clutter is still clutter whether it is in storage or on your shelves.

Once you have completed the first seven steps of the decluttering process, now consider if there are any clever ways you can improve the storage and sorting of the items you have kept, to ensure they stay as organised as possible. This does not have to be high-end designer storage - be creative.

Try repurposing and reusing some of the items I have listed.

www.naomifindlay.com/bookbonus access to periscope videos

chapter 4

ROOM BY ROOM CLUTTER CLEANSE

"Remember that the investment you make now in keeping your house clean and clutter-free will reap rewards."

Naomi Findlay PhD

Below is a more focused guide packed with some of my top tips for getting rid of clutter by working your way through you house, room by room.

BEDROOM

Your bedroom should be a place of relaxation and retreat where comfort is top priority - but clutter quite often creeps in here and decides to stay!

If space is limited, use a tallboy with eight drawers rather than a chest to maximise the use of vertical space.

Your bedside table should have shelving and at least one drawer to stow personal items in.

Think outside the square. Use stationary dividers in your bedside drawers to divide up the space and keep things ordered.

If there is no room for a bedside table, get a long floating shelf installed above the bed to use instead.

Use under bed storage to store seasonal clothes.

Use the inside of the wardrobe door for hooks to hold belts, scarves and jewellery. If there is no space on the inside, use decorative hooks on the side of the wardrobe and display your most chic handbags and accessories.

As far as clothes are concerned, if you have not worn it for two seasons then it goes in the charity bin straight away. Then use a hanger system to determine which clothes you use the most.

To keep you motivated; make a pledge to yourself, "I will not buy another item of clothing or accessory for myself until I have sorted my wardrobe". That is sure to get you moving!

If your linen press is too small and your linen is choking up your clothes space, try a chest or trunk at the end of the bed to act as a bed ottoman and a linen storage space too.

You can use the top of your wardrobe for additional storage, as long as the items are stored in matching containers that have lids that close.

If you really get into it maybe create a vision board of how you ideally want your bedroom to look. Once it is decluttered and organised you can start on restyling it!

LIVING SPACE

A living area is often one of your most-used rooms for recreation and relaxation in a home. Given this, it can sometimes get a bit messy and suffer from a lack of order.

Here are some tips to help you maintain order and organisation in your living space.

1. Organise different areas of your living room depending on what activities go on in these areas.

   Consider what activities actually occur in that room. I would think more than four might be a few too many for one space, unless it is planned very well. Many of my clients list activities such as watching TV, talking, reading and relaxing.

   You now need to identify where each activity occurs in the room and what you need to have nearby to make the activity pleasurable and easy to clear up afterwards.

   For example, if you love reading your favourite interiors magazine in your favourite chair at night with a drink, it makes sense that you will need a lamp, table, cushion and somewhere nearby for the magazines to be stored.

   Similarly, you would need to have your remotes and Foxtel program near to where you love to watch the TV. By storing the items that you need for each activity you will find that you spend less time putting things away and your living space will feel more organised overall.

2. Keep your cables under control. Nothing screams mess, dust and disaster more than tangled, messy, exposed power and audiovisual cables.

There are a lot of gadgets on the market to help you keep these in order, however simple cable ties will often do the trick. Use them to group your cables together and keep them neat.

3. Create a play zone. If you have children, rather than have all the toys sprawled across the living space, create an area that is dedicated to toys.

   That way you can more easily contain them in one place, as well as keep the kids happy that they get to play where everyone else is hanging out, rather than in their rooms.

4. Keep current issues of magazines in a woven basket near the couch for access and easy reading. Clean it out every few months so it doesn't become overcrowded.

5. Small trinkets and odds and ends are usually not that appealing to the eye. If there are things you do not want to get rid of, store them in matching boxes with the lids on, in a shelved area.

6. If your lounge room is big enough, create a working library, where there are some comfortable seats, and shelving for all your books and magazines.

7. Cluttered horizontal spaces can be very distracting and messy to the eye. If your side tables are cluttered with too many family portraits, move them off and make a family photo wall instead. There are loads of ways to bring it together and make it look great.

Here are a few ideas:

- Convert all your pictures to black and white.
- Use the same coloured frames of different shapes and sizes.
- Place all your photos in only one style frame.
- Using these simple strategies will help give your living space a functional and visual edge.

BATHROOMS

Remember if you do not use it in this space it does NOT belong here.

If space is limited go for a large mirrored cabinet, ideally recessed into the wall.

If you have open shelves you can use these to stow smaller items, making sure they are in identical containers. If the items are "messy" to look at, use frosted or opaque containers to minimise the visual clutter.

Use hooks on the back of the door for robes and towels to give you extra hanging space.

When it comes to your makeup and skincare, DON'T store like with like. This may work for hair elastics and soap but not for makeup.

For example, is there ever a time where you have used / worn all of your eye shadows at once? Following the principle of zoning, the makeup that you use most often should be stored together so it can be used together. Items used less often or for special occasions should then be stored together, but separately to the everyday items.

This will save you a lot of time each day as you will not be scrambling around looking for your favourite lip gloss or moisturiser. Everything you need for your daily routine will be in one place.

If you have multiple "nearly finished" toiletries that you have moved on from, get them out and either use them in the next week or throw them out!

KITCHENS

As you move through the kitchen make sure you address the following:

Look at how you stack your dinnerware. Try and stack your plates and bowls in quantities that you use. For example, if you have a family of four and tend to use four or five plates to serve up and eat dinner, have all dinnerware in stacks of five. What do you use? I know with a family of six, I use seven plates at a time.

Try the following stacking system: Stack your bowls inside one another with the largest at the bottom. Stack your plates together too.

Ditch the unloved and rarely used wedding gifts!

If the shelves inside your cupboards are quite high, look at using shelf inserts to halve the height of each shelf and hence double your shelf space. This means less lifting and moving of plates and bowls to get to what you want.

Take note of what you use regularly - you will be surprised at how limited your usage of kitchen items is on a day-to-day basis. This will not only help you with your Declutter Dash but it will also help you prioritise your kitchen organisation.

Be quick and smart when you hit your pantry by asking the following questions:

- Is it in date?
- Is it in good condition?
- How does it smell and look?
- Have I used it in the last six months and will it keep for another six months?
- Does it need repackaging?
- Does everything have a label (if necessary)?
- Are all like things stored together? Here are a few categories you could use when grouping things together: school snacks; baking goods; sauces and dressings; breakfast needs and spreads; tea and coffee; and treats.

Everyone I have ever met has a "bits/junk" drawer in the kitchen – even me! This drawer should only have items that belong to the kitchen. If it is not used for cooking, cleaning or eating then it does not belong and you need to find a new home for it or throw it out!

And make sure you leave no space in the kitchen untouched - even under the sink! Start by moving anything you use sporadically to the garage or pantry and throwing out anything rusted, crusted, or congealed. Consider a pull-out garbage bin on gliders, or door attachments to hold sponges, brushes, and plastic wrap and aluminium foil. A plastic caddy can be used to contain all your cleaning products and supplies on one side of the space under the sink, giving you room to put the garbage bin (if this is where it lives) on the other side.

"Take note of what you use regularly – you will be surprised at how limited your usage of some items is on a day-to-day basis."

Naomi Findlay PhD

Quick tips:

- For all of the contents in your kitchen plan it around your work zones: cooking, eating, cleaning and food storage. Similarly, store things according to their function.

- Special occasion serving ware such as dinner plates and glassware does not need to be in an easy access location.

- Let usage dictate storage. Divide your space into 'essentials', 'useful' and 'luxury' and categorise items and their accessibility based on what category they fall into. Keep frequently used cookware easily at hand. Stow things you use every now and then, like muffin tins and cookie sheets, in a less accessible cabinet. Those that are used only once or twice a year should not occupy valuable real estate – you can store them in an out-of-the-way cupboard or even in the garage.

- Consider putting a notice board or a white board on the inside of cupboard or pantry doors.

- Don't allow things from all over the house to find a permanent home in the kitchen and don't let the kitchen bench be the dumping ground for all your paperwork or unopened mail.

- Have a shopping list in the kitchen at all times - each time a product runs out, add it straight to the list. Better still, Woolworths have an app that allows you to scan the barcode and add it straight to your shopping list.

- If there is truly nowhere else in your house for your paperwork, bills, and notes to be kept, try this to help keep them under control. Use one magazine file or A5 clipboard for each "category", ie. each child; bills; work; sporting etc. All the notes that are relevant to that activity or person that cannot be thrown out should be placed into this file/ board rather than all over the fridge or counter top. Another great way to conquer this is to go online by scanning your essential notes and paperwork. This will not only keep your kitchen looking good, but it will make sure you have round-the-clock access to the items on your smartphone.

KEEPING CLUTTER-FREE

You have put a lot of work into making your property clutter-free, but how do you keep it that way?

Here are some sure-fire strategies that will help you develop a plan to maintain a low clutter environment for the duration of the property preparation as well as the sale campaign.

- Try and think before you bring extra items into the home.

- Do a regular declutter run, leaving no stone unturned. If you do this each day it should not take you more than 15-20 minutes – effectively doing a Declutter Dash each night. This does NOT mean cleaning up after dinner and doing the dishes, this involves moving from one end of the home to the other to remove surface clutter before it gets too much. If you find 15 minutes is not long enough, you either haven't decluttered well in the first place or you have not kept on top of the clutter since.

To complete your nightly Declutter Dash, try the following:

- Grab an empty washing basket and start at one end of the home.

- Put away everything that has been left lying out in each room. If it does not have a home there and you can't easily find one, then it does not belong in that room. Put it in the basket and take it with you until you reach the room where it belongs, then put it away.

Get the kids involved and make it fun! Here are a couple of examples of how you can do that:

- Make it a fun competition. Each night at a specific time have a game to see who can pack away the clutter in their room first, possibly with a reward attached.

- For older kids, incorporate it into the chores they have to complete to earn their pocket money.

- For younger kids, you could make it a game of putting the toys "to bed".

- Avoid shopping for household and clothing items. Buy only essential items.

- Make the most of online options for your bills and notices, including the school newsletter.

- Think before you print. There are so many things we print out from our email accounts and internet that are not necessary. Write important details into a diary instead if you need it in hard copy.

- You should never handle things more than two times. For example, when you open the mail decide whether it gets recycled, or dealt with immediately (bill paid or filed away), thus only being handled once. Alternatively if the mail is something you need to action later, it goes to a "deal with later" file, in which case it is handled a second time and then filed.

Another example of the above principle is when you come home. Jackets and shoes are put away immediately into their designated area (closet, coat rack...), unless there are compelling reasons to do otherwise, such as your hands are full of groceries and you need to carry them into the kitchen. In this case, the shoes are kicked off and handled a second time - once you put the groceries down you go back and put the shoes away.

Remember that the investment you make now in keeping your house clean and clutter-free will reap rewards. You will minimise the chances of becoming overwhelmed by clutter again and having to start back at ground zero.

- Some of us love lists and putting pen to paper, while others are completely comfortable with the world of the cloud and are happy to have a lot of their decluttering online. Below are some of my favourite apps that help me eliminate day-to-day clutter in my life.

  - Wunderlust
  - Asana
  - Evertone
  - Online shopping app
  - Google apps - including Google calendar
  - Lastpass

KEEPING CLUTTER-FREE WITH KIDS

Keeping your newly decluttered home tidy and organised can be even more difficult when you have kids. Following my tips will help keep you moving in the right direction.

* Find a motivation and define a reward for both you and your kids to keep the house tidy and clutter-free.

* In order to have a somewhat tidy home with kids, everything needs to have a place to be returned to. Otherwise when you tidy and organise you are simply shifting clutter from one place to the next.

* Be consistent! Day-to-day clutter and mess from family life can seem overwhelming if you let it build up, so it is important to dedicate some time each day to this effort. Why not do a nightly Declutter Dash, after your kids have gone to bed. Investing this small amount of time each night will hold you in good stead for the next day.

* Empower the kids to help. You know your children better than anyone – use what makes them tick to get them involved. Funnily enough, my seven-year-old daughter loves arranging and re-arranging her room with cushions and art and accessories (not sure how that happened!). To get her on board I have sold her on the virtues and aesthetic appeal of a clutter-free room. With younger children this is not as easy, but they are never too young to start learning new habits!

* A great technique to try is the "left out basket". Each child (I have four) has a "left out basket" and each night when I am whipping around the house for one final sweep, anything

they have left out gets transferred to their basket. Each time the left out basket gets full, they have to take it into their room and sift through the contents - kind of like their own Declutter Dash!

- There are so many ways you can stay organised in the home with a family and look stylish at the same time. My final tip is BE REAL! Kids are kids and family life and fun is to be treasured. Think about trying one new strategy each month to help you stay organised during your sale campaign and find what works for you and your family!

www.naomifindlay.com/bookbonus voucher $50 bootcamp and boxlabels

chapter 5

PROPERTY MAINTENENCE AND UPGRADES

PROPERTY MAINTAINENCE AND UPGRADES

After working for years in the property and styling industry, I have learnt that the top turn-offs for buyers when they are looking at a property are odours, dark spaces, ill repair and dirty properties.

Increasing the value of your property in the eyes of a buyer is directly related to the level of repair and maintenance the property requires -both in the short and long term.

With this in mind it is essential your place is presented in a manner that helps the buyer think the property is well cared for, well maintained, and low maintenance to live in.

For example if you have a lovely bush setting at the rear of the property, the last thing a buyer wants to see is a pool full of leaves or an outdoor living space whose gutters are blocked and showing signs of rust.

MAINTENANCE VERSUS UPGRADES

Home staging is NOT RENOVATING! It is certainly fair to say that some small maintenance and improvement tasks can fall under the umbrella of home staging, but ripping out and replacing a bathroom or kitchen is beyond the scope of this process. Such major tasks fall into the realm of renovating for profit or house flipping.

However, maintenance issues must be addressed otherwise buyers see each outstanding maintenance item as another reason to knock down the sale price of your property. Don't give buyers any reason to do this.

Common maintenance tasks can include:

- decks that need oiling;
- taps that leak;
- windows that are hard to open;
- torn fly screens;
- doors that do not shut properly;
- greasy hand marks on the walls;
- pet mess in the outdoor areas;
- gardens that need weeding and mulching; and
- driveways and footpaths that have mould and moss on them.

There are times where upgrading areas of a house can be a great way to add extra value to the property. However, you need to be extremely careful that you:

- don't over-capitalise on the upgrade you do.
- only complete upgrades that will add value to the home - don't complete ones simply because they have been on your "wish list" for a long time; and
- don't inject too much individual style into the upgrade.

When you are considering whether to upgrade an area of your property, it pays to do your research and complete the following steps before you spend any of your hard-earned cash.

1. Consult with an expert in your area. Seek advice from a professional home stager or real estate agent about the proposed upgrades. Get their perspective on what you are planning - is it something that buyers in your target market expect, or could you run the risk of not gaining any more money at sale time?

2. Clearly establish how much the entire upgrade will cost. Make sure you do the numbers and account for all the finishing touches, as well as a "blow-out" budget. Once you have the costs finalised, revisit your property research and explore whether your proposed upgrade will realise a threefold profit when the property is sold. For example, if you are going to invest $10,000 in a new bathroom, will it make you an additional $25,000 to $30,000? If not, you need to consider whether the upgrade is worth the time and effort.

3. If you have completed all your research and still want to go ahead with the upgrade, it is essential to make sure you complete the work with the target market in mind, rather

than to your tastes. Remember - the property is no longer a home, it is a product that is not about you. When you are working out the design and choosing the finishes for your proposed upgrade, make sure the space will appeal to at least 80% of your target market without polarising any of them.

4. Think laterally! An upgrade does not always have to mean a major renovation - it could be as simple as changing door handles or painting a splash back. Consult an independent third party to help you stay focused on the big picture of maximising the sale price of your property without breaking your staging budget.

HOW TO FIND AND KEEP TRADIES

Hands down I owe a huge part of my renovation and house flipping success to a fantastic team of tradies. The team has everything from core elements such as builders, plumber and electricians, to surveyors, town planners, property developers, estate agents, stone masons and great suppliers to name just a few.

There are plenty of mainstream ways to find tradies; the internet, new apps, advertising etc, and there is naturally an important due diligence process that you MUST follow that involves checking licences and insurance before you engage a trade.

But in this next section I am going to share with you my secrets to finding and keeping good tradies.

Many of these things seem pure common sense when I write them down, but it appears we sometimes overlook these items when we are looking for and working with tradies.

FINDING THEM

Ask other tradies. If you are already working with a good team and want to add to it, ask the tradies you are working with for their recommendations. Like attracts like, so if you like the tradies you have, more than likely you will like the tradies they enjoy working with too.

Meet with the tradies before you get them onsite; offer to meet them on one of their job sites. This will allow you to get a feel for them and also get an idea of how they work.

For me it is very simple. If they look me in the eye, shake my hand firmly, can hold a respectful conversation with me about the work they do, then we are off to a good start.

I generally ask them about the jobs they have on at the moment, who is in their team, what their lead times are and specifics about the task that I am keen to have them work on.

I also find out who they know in the industry as cross-checking them with other tradies is a great way to get honest feedback.

Then …. give them a shot. Using a tradie once does not mean they are yours forever. On the first job, make sure you communicate with them, extremely clearly, in multiple mediums.

Call them to tell them what you want done, meet them on site to show them and have the instructions and diagrams of what you want done written and stuck on the walls of the job. Then leave them to it, don't micromanage them or watch them work! That shows NO trust.

"There are times where upgrading areas of a house can be a great way to add extra value to the property."

Naomi Findlay PhD

KEEPING YOUR TEAM HAPPY AND PRODUCTIVE

This is all about respect: respect for their skill, their trade and most importantly, them as people.

How do you do this? Follow these simple lessons, that apply everywhere in life.

When I go on site I greet every tradie with a handshake or a kiss (if I'm particularly familiar with them!), calling them by name. If I see someone on site I don't know, I always introduce myself and find out their name.

If I arrive to site with a coffee, I will always bring drinks for the tradies on site as well.

Every day, I tell them how happy I am with the job (as long as I am). If I am not happy about something, I seek to understand before I seek to be understood.

I pay VERY quickly! Inspect the job as soon as it is complete and then you will be ready to pay as soon as that invoice comes in. I never leave a tradie to wait for payment.

I get dirty! When required I join my tradies to demonstrate and to clean up.

Show an interest in what they do and why; most tradies are so keen to share their knowledge they are just waiting for someone to ask.

Involve the tradies in the project; feeling part of a team can make all the difference.

Plan well. Tradies are constantly being asked to do things at the drop of a hat. Be the stand-out client and book them as much in advance as you can.

Enjoy your tradies. It is so great to be part of a great team of tradies, and it can be such a joy to be onsite with a great team!

SAVING ON TRADIES

Good tradespeople are worth their weight in gold! When renovating, an expert tradie can truly make all the difference in coming in or above budget.

Time is money for tradies, so if you're not working on a fixed price quote, every hour tradies spend on site is an hour you're being charged for!

Below are four tips to help save time for your tradies and in turn save money! They may look small, but over a large job these little things really add up.

1. Avoid the setting up and packing up. When tradies start and finish work there is a substantial amount of setting up and packing up that needs to get done. In some cases, if the worksite is not deemed secure, tradies will have to unpack their tools from their truck daily. One great way to save on this one-hour task is to provide your tradies with a locked space on site they can securely store their tools in. This could be an unused room, lawn locker or garage. Give the key to the tradies so they know their tools are safe when they are off-site.

2. Clean the site. A dirty site slows work down. But you don't want to be paying your tradie to clean it - this is a total waste of your budget! Pitch in and get active; simply picking up rubbish and sweeping every few days can make a world of difference to the pace of work, efficiency and safety.

3. Be the site PA. Let your tradie know you are able to do some of the legwork for them, for example picking up supplies, arranging deliveries or checking stock availability. The more time your tradies spend on the phone, the less time they are on the tools! There are obviously many things that your tradies will not be able to delegate to you, but you will be amazed at how many little jobs you can take off their hands.

1. Get dirty. There are a lot of jobs during a renovation that can be done by even the most unskilled renovator, like digging holes and moving dirt. So roll up those sleeves and give it a go!

Obviously it is essential to listen to your tradies and work within the workplace health and safety boundaries (which they will be able to guide you on). But in most cases you will find your tradies welcome the extra help! And believe me, I can tell you from my own personal experience that my time spent cleaning a site, digging postholes and lugging timber has been very warmly received!

MANAGING YOUR PROPERTY PROJECT

A well-managed property project is one of the best ways to have a stress-free project. For me, the key to this is organisation, communication, forward planning and documentation.

Here are my top tips to make your project go as smoothly as possible.

1. Have a direction of where you are heading. Managing a renovation project is like leading a team. It is essential to know where you want the project to end up. For example, don't have your builders move walls one day and then ask them to change the walls two days later. It will cost you tenfold.

2. Once you know where you are going, it is essential that you forward plan. Many things take time to get on-site: frames, garage doors, mixers and tiles, just to name a few. This also applies to your tradespeople. Calling a plumber for work you want completed the next day - that is not a true emergency - is a recipe for a poor working relationship.

    Forward planning the whole renovation and allowing one day breathing space between your tradies is essential. For example, once the plumbers have roughed in the bathroom and it is sheeted by the builder, plan to have the waterproofer in a day later. This will mean that if either of the previous tradies run late or run into difficulty, your whole timeline will not be derailed. Turning away a tradie on a day they were booked in may mean waiting a week or so until they can get back to your job. If you are looking for a tight and quick renovation, this can spell disaster.

3. You have your direction and you have forward planned your materials and tradies, now you need to make sure you've

communicated this with everyone who needs to know. There are many software packages that can help with project management (such as Estate Planner), or you can keep it simple with a notebook and pen.

Give your tradies as much notice as possible. It is not unusual for me to book my electrician four weeks in advance. This allows him time to plan his work and make sure that when the date rolls around, my project is at the front of the queue.

Simple strategies such as having plans and task lists for each tradie laminated and adhered to the walls can be a great way to make sure that your tradies have everything they need when they arrive on site. Also arrange at least twice-weekly site meetings to assess the progress, your tradies' needs and their stock levels. These strategies will help keep your plan and direction on track.

Everyone is busy so make sure that you give your tradies and suppliers timely follow-ups and reminders of what you have previously arranged with them. Most tradies really appreciate this communication.By making sure you show due diligence in regard to these three essential elements, you are well on your way to managing your project successfully.

MANAGING YOUR PROJECT BUDGET

Whether you are renovating/upgrading for profit to sell or value add or to stay in your home, your budget should be a primary driver for all renovators. Projecting your budget, keeping to budget and always knowing how you're tracking is essential.

The first step is to have a detailed list of the costs that will be incurred during your renovation. Ideally this would be broken down, element by element. For example, rather than one element being demolition, have this broken down into: labour for demolition, rubbish removal, site clean-up, disposal of hazardous materials (if applicable), etc. Breaking the budget down will allow you to better determine as you progress through the project how well you are tracking and if you are on target to make budget.

Many people ask me where I get the numbers from for my budget categories. If you have never renovated before this can be difficult.

So to start off, ask your tradies lots of questions. Use their expertise to project anticipated costs for all facets of the renovation. Using this method once you have a few renovations under your belt will ensure you have a clear and detailed breakdown of what past projects have cost and allow you to project your future budgets with confidence.

Without doubt, every renovation project has an unexpected surprise. At the onset it is essential that you factor a buffer into the budget. There are various opinions on how much this should be, "but no lower than 10-15% of the total projected budget is a good place to start". This will mean when an unexpected expense occurs it does not derail your budget.

It is all well and good to have a budget, but now you need to stick to it. To do this the budget needs constant attention. "At least twice a week you need to assess what has been spent on all facets of the project, including holding costs."

Using a simple program such as Microsoft Excel or similar means you can track your expenditure on a spreadsheet and see if there are any variations from the expected.

Each time you complete this task you need to collate any variations. This will help shape your future decisions, giving you the best possible chance to stay on budget and on target for a successful renovation.

chapter 6

APPLYING THE MECHANISMS OF HOME STAGING

APPLYING THE MECHANISMS OF HOME STAGING

I've already gone over the principles and mechanisms of how home staging works, as well as the things you need to think about when it comes to preparing your property for sale.

Now I want to help you apply these items.

Property presentation

THE LAW OF ATTRACTION VS. DISTRACTION

When it comes to selling your property, you want to attract - not distract - a buyer! And with statistics telling us that a buyer's first impression is made in the first two minutes of a viewing, while the average open house inspection takes 12-20 minutes, time has never been so critical.

When you think about it, 12-20 minutes is a short period of time to get through a three to four-bedroom home.

It is a rare case (and I have only had a few of these in my time) where there are absolutely no positive features in a property, in which case it is totally okay to distract a buyer through home staging!

However, in nearly all cases it is essential that you allow the highlights of the property to shine through and provide as little stimulus as possible to distract a buyer.

Here are some of the top causes of unwanted distraction when inspecting a property for sale:

ODOURS

Bad odours have been reported as the number one turn-off for buyers. Whether this is smoke, pets, dampness, food or other unpleasant odours, they are all an unwanted distraction for a buyer.

Often , the people who live in a property that has an odour cannot smell it, so be brave and ask your stylist, estate agent or an honest family member / friend if there are any unwanted smells. Most importantly, take note and get onto their eradication as soon as possible; odours can often take some time and effort to shift.

LIGHTS

Poor lighting is a huge distraction for buyers. If your home lacks natural light then make sure you inject a good dose of additional and accent lighting into the space before an open house inspection.

MUSIC

Music can be a great mood setter, but it can also cause distraction if it is too loud or too polarising in its style. If in doubt have no music at all, it is a much safer option.

PERSONAL EFFECTS

Having photos all over the walls, trophies on shelves, and your clothes, toiletries and shoes out for all to see means a buyer is spending too much time wondering who you are and not enough time taking the property in!

Make sure you remove as many personal effects as you can before your open house.

STYLING

When styling a property for sale, it is critical that the styling embellishes the property and not distracts from it. Never make the styling too targeted to a certain audience and try not to let the styling drown out the features of the property.

Wherever possible, let your furniture float; in other words, leave some space around your key pieces such as sofas. You may think pushing your sofa up against the wall will make the room feel and look bigger, when in fact the opposite is usually the case. Space between the wall and your furniture implies you have more than enough room to fit everything in.

Furniture that is raised up off the floor (sofas, coffee tables, armchairs with legs) also adds to the feeling of spaciousness.

Use clever furniture such as dining tables that slide out to create extra seating only when necessary, or ottomans with storage inside to pack away items that could make your room look cluttered, and therefore smaller.

Create the illusion of more height in your room by drawing the eye upwards - your room will immediately feel more spacious. You can do this by painting the ceiling only in a bold hue. Or you could install long (almost ceiling to floor) drapes over your windows, even if the windows are small. The vertical length of the drapes will draw the eye upwards. But make sure you keep the drapes the same colour as the walls to avoid creating too much contrast. A wall of floor-to-ceiling shelving will also create the illusion of height.

Let as much natural light into a room as possible as it helps open up a space.

Avoid using busy patterns in your floor rug in a small room; this will only increase the feeling of clutter. Instead use a plain colour to visually expand the room.

Be clever with your choice of lighting by considering it from a functional and mood perspective. You can do this by adding an additional layer to your standard room lighting with a floor or table lamp.

Avoid busyness - multiple contrasting design features in a small space can make it look fussy and crowded.

When holding an open house inspection, having a nicely-styled home can be the difference between a quick and profitable sale versus months, if not years, on the market.

It's important that potential buyers can imagine themselves in your home, so decluttering, de-personalising and neutralising the colour palette are vital ways for getting a timely sale.

BE A SHOW-OFF

When open house comes along, make sure your house is at its finest. All your preparation is wasted if you're not in tip top shape on the actual day it counts!

Turn all the lights on, have the house heated or cooled to the most comfortable temperature, have as much natural light as possible and make sure all your cushions, throws and homewares are placed correctly. Don't start baking or brewing though, as for some potential buyers that is just a little too staged!

"When open house comes along, make sure your house is at its finest. All your preparation is wasted if you're not in tip top shape on the actual day it counts!"

Naomi Findlay PhD

SHOWCASE YOUR KITCHEN ASSET

It is common knowledge that there are some big ticket items or drawcards when it comes to selling your property; kitchens, bathrooms, outdoor living areas and, depending on the location, car parking are among the major players.

So it goes without saying that you need to focus on your assets and make sure they are singing in tune with the calibre of property you are presenting to the market. What makes or breaks the way a kitchen is presented?

First let's consider what you are trying to sell when staging and styling the kitchen space; it could be any or all of the following:

1. A cook's kitchen.
2. An entertainer's kitchen.
3. A family kitchen.
4. A kitchen perfect for a takeaway food lover.

One thing is certain, we are NOT trying to sell the image or vision of:

1. A hard to maintain kitchen.
2. A kitchen that needs upgrading.
3. A kitchen with little storage.
4. A kitchen that doesn't accommodate entertaining.

Regardless of the vision you are wanting to create for your kitchen (this will be largely dependent on the buyer or target market's demographic), here are my failsafe tips to making sure that your kitchen shines on open day.

1. Gut it - Step one is undoubtedly getting stuck into removing anything from your kitchen that it is not essential to have in the house during the sale process. This includes everything from the serving ware that is only used at Christmas to the chocolate fountain that comes out every Easter and the slow

cooker that never sees the light of day except in the coldest month of the year. Use this new-found cupboard space to clear your benches of all the day-to-day clutter that accumulates in your kitchen. Everything that is in your kitchen needs to have a home in a cupboard or a drawer, NOT on your kitchen bench.

Next stop, the pantry. Remove all out-of-date or nearly empty packets; at least a third of the pantry's contents needs to be removed and thrown out or stored off site.

It is essential that the pantry and cupboards look like there is room to move and that your storage in the kitchen is certainly not at capacity.

2. Clean it - All the things most people don't get a chance to attend to must be sparkling! These include:

- Range hood.
- Oven.
- Behind and under the fridge.
- Microwave pocket.
- Under the dishwasher.
- Pendant lights.
- Skylight.

1. Organise it - You have gone to the trouble of emptying and cleaning the kitchen so go the extra mile and organise it as you put the contents back in. This is especially important in kitchens that have opaque glass cupboard fronts or open shelving where the contents are on display.

Consider the heights and colours of the items when putting them away, as well as the position of the labels. A well-organised cupboard promotes the concept of a well-maintained, well cared for and well-loved kitchen - an ideal impression to be giving a buyer.

2. Introduce life and colour - The modern kitchen is no longer a pure utility space. It is an integrated living space in the home and hence it needs to be dressed to feel that way! Utilise:

- Flowers - simple and one type of flower or mixed foliage rather than a traditional bouquet.
- Herbs or terrariums - make sure they are fresh and thriving.
- Cook books - nothing gives life to a space like books and the kitchen is no exception. Choose your best books to adorn a shelf or as a stack on the bench.
- Fruit - in a monochrome manner, not a mixed bunch.
- If you have any showpiece and in vogue appliances like a "Kitchen Aide" mixer or amazing coffee machine, then certainly show them off. But as a general rule, limit it to one bench top appliance, and only if you have a large amount of kitchen bench space.

3. Showcase its capacity - If you have an eat-in or breakfast bar facility in the kitchen, don't assume that everyone will notice it unless you show them. Do this by making sure there is seating on show in this space.

4. Maintain it! - Once all this hard work is done, develop a strategy to maintain it for the sale period.

LOCATION, LOCATION, LOCATION

When it comes to real estate, it's all about location and placement.

But when it comes to successfully staging a home to sell for the highest possible price, the importance of location applies to more than just the street address.

The placement of your furniture and accessories can make or break a room and potentially even a sale.

The look and feel of a space is created by the way the various items in that room are positioned - put them in the wrong spots and you can instantly diminish the overall appearance of the area, regardless of whether the items individually are stylish and on-trend.

Good placement however will have the opposite effect, to the point where even less attractive furniture located correctly around the room can produce amazing results.

The crucial element in solving the placement puzzle is balance. The furniture and accessories should make the room flow, be in proportion to the space and harmoniously connect with each other and the purpose of the area.

Learning to read a room - assessing its physical elements like size, shape and architectural features - will help you know how to best arrange the items within it to be functional and look fabulous as well.

Flow is also important - the way you move through a room is determined and directed by the placement of the furniture within it. You want the furniture to help a person utilise the space in the best means possible to fit the purpose of the room - not hinder them by making them feel like it is always in the way.

Never place large furniture near a door or in a walkway where it will block the natural path you would take through the room. You should be able to easily walk through a room without tripping over objects or constantly deviating your path to go around items of furniture.

The flow of a room can also relate to the way the most used items in a room - such as the TV, lounge and coffee table - are placed in relation to each other to encourage natural interactions. Good flow creates positive impressions and allows for flexibility within your spaces.

Thankfully, most rooms within a property can be fitted into one of five different shape categories - rectangle, long and narrow, square, L-shaped and angular. If you identify the shape of the room, you can apply the techniques that have been proven time and again to work best for that shape.

SHAPE UP: ROOM FOR SQUARES

The way you place furniture in a square room can make or break it. You may have great furniture and a great space, but if you don't get it right you will have no hope of achieving the balance and harmony that a space needs in order to create a good impression.

The three things to remember about any space are:

1. Your traffic zones.
2. How you are going to move around the space.
3. How you are going to use the space.

Sometime a square room can feel a little boring and lack dynamic, so it is important that once you have identified the main feature of the room, for example a fireplace or a large bay window, you then make sure it is the room's shining star.

If there is no focal point, create one by employing a huge piece of art to help create some pizzazz in the space or by including a feature piece of furniture (throne, anyone?).

Another way to break up the regularity of the room is to make sure the eye has some vertical interest to follow in the space. Make sure that there are elements of the room that make the eye lift from the furniture to the lighting. Typical ways to achieve this effect are through the arrangement of large accessories, flowers or lamps that encourage a person's gaze upwards, or by using pendant lights to catch their attention.

Regularity and symmetry can also be an asset if you do it right. Don't be frightened to enhance the squareness of the space by duplicating the symmetry with the furniture, such as by placing two identical lounges opposite each other. The effect will obviously depend on what else is in the space, but deliberate symmetry can sharpen the room.

Remember you can also work the diagonals in a square room, either by softening the corners with furniture or accessories to change perception of the room shape or by pushing the symmetry with the midline drawn from corner to corner, rather than wall to wall.

All of these tips will help bring some movement and excitement into a square room.

HOW TO FURNISH A RECTANGULAR ROOM

Room shapes and the placement of furniture within them have a huge impact on how people perceive the space. A rectangular room is fairly common, but you'd be surprised at how easy it is to make mistakes.

Surprisingly, large rectangular rooms cause as many issues as smaller rooms. The biggest mistake people make with a large rectangular room is that they treat it as one space. But beware: if it isn't a ballroom, it should have different zones.

Break the room up into conversation spaces or areas. In a living room this might be a TV area and a reading area; in a bedroom it could be a sleep zone and a study area.

First take into account the size of the room and the position of the entryway and thoroughfare before choosing where to put a zone.

Windows and lighting may also dictate where you can put certain items of furniture: reflection off a TV or computer screen is bad for your eyesight and that leather upholstered armchair isn't going to age well in the hot sunny spot.

Choose furniture or groups of furniture that are in proportion with the zone. If your favourite lamp and side table pairing is dwarfed by the zone you've allocated for it, choose another zone or choose another combination of furniture that better fits the space.

If your rectangular room is narrow, there are a few tricks you can use to make it look less elongated. Either widen the long sides, for example using light, light colours or mirrors, or shorten the far sides with well-placed pieces of furniture or styling elements that reduce the length of the room.

A big but long room can handle some unusual furniture placement, for example settings placed perpendicular to the thoroughfare and walls, to break the tunnel-like feel of the room.

Don't forget you can use the floor space to indicate where zones begin and end. Use a large floor rug to contain the entertainment zone while leaving the rest of the room uncovered to denote another area.

HOW TO MAKE A SMALL ROOM LOOK BIG

Although bold colours on walls can look sensational, avoid them at all costs in a small room that you are wanting to appear larger. Stick to light and bright hues to maximise the feeling of space and help the walls 'recede'.

Use mirrors. Mirrors not only bounce light around the room making it feel larger, they also instantly double the space by playing tricks on the eye. In a very small room such as toilet or laundry, mirror the entire ceiling to open up the space and create a "skylight".

LIGHTING MAKES A ROOM COME ALIVE!

There is more to successful home staging than just choosing a colour scheme, working out how to furnish and decorate a space and examining its physical characteristics and functionality. The way a room smells, feels to the touch and even the way it sounds, all have an influence on how a person interacts with a space.

Most notably though, the way a room looks has a defining effect on the way a person feels about that space - and one of the easiest and most common methods of altering a room's appearance is through lighting.

It is crucial that consideration is given to the way a room is currently being lit when you are preparing to redesign or style the space.

Look at the light sources - are they natural (windows, doorways, skylights) or man-made (electric lights)?

Do they highlight the features of the room or do they draw a person's eye to the wrong elements?

Is there enough light for the purpose of the room - can you cook / read / put on your makeup / paint etc effectively with the existing amount of light?

Depending on the lights you choose, you can either make them fade into the background as they bring another element within the room to life - or they can become a feature themselves, with the dual purpose of looking good and increasing visibility.

The lighting used in a room can change its mood in a second. The right lights can make a cold room feel warmer and cosier, while the wrong selection of lighting could make a modern, minimalist room seem stark and impersonal.

When selecting your lights consider the following points:

- Is this light for function or for feature? What is its function or what are you making a feature of? Are you wanting to read with it or is it to enhance the texture look of a wall?

- What sort of space do you have available? Can you use a floor lamp or will you need to place a table lamp on an existing piece of furniture?

- What level would you like the lighting? Floor or ground level, eye level or above head height?

- What type of light do you want to use in the space? Cool light or a warm light? Light bulbs can be purchased off the shelf that throw different hues when turned on. Your choice of light colour will greatly depend on the other lighting in the space, the colours and feel of the space and the function of the space.

Answering these four simple questions will be a great start to steering you in the right direction; the final piece of the puzzle is choosing a light that works with your style and existing decor.

List to clichés to avoid:

CLICHES TO AVOID

What sells a house? A home that is well presented, well priced and effectively marketed will sell! So to sell your home you need to make sure that you have:

- Undertaken thorough and objective research into what your property is worth, to ensure you are well priced.
- Enlisted the expertise of a good real estate agent.
- Presented your property so that its highlights are showcased and buyers can inspect it without distractions.

Gone are the days where a simple declutter and clean is all that is needed to present your home for sale.

Buyers are more and more sophisticated and expect a much higher level of presentation than ever before. This being said, there is such a fine line between presenting your home for sale to enhance its highlights and over-staging your home.

What is wrong with over-staging your property? When you cross the line between presenting a well maintained and inviting space and presenting a home that has cliché after cliché, you run the risk of polarising your buyers. Or worse still, distracting them so much with all your "staging clichés" that they neglect to see all the amazing aspects that your property has to offer.

To help you avoid this pitfall here are some of the top staging clichés to be avoided:

- Filling the bath or spa with water, bubbles or rose petals.
- Rose and champagne on the end of the bed.
- Pillows on point in the bedroom or living spaces.
- Cookies baking in the oven. Unless you are going to be feeding the buyers, don't distract them by making them hungry.
- Setting the table for a three-course meal.

- Reading glasses open on a book by a reading chair.
- Empty saucepans on the cook top to try and give the "gourmet kitchen" feel.
- The throw rug randomly thrown across the ottoman or lounge.
- Overusing supermarket scents and air fresheners.

While I am a strong advocate for styling your home for sale and creating a home that is inviting and paints the picture of the lifestyle it can offer a buyer, I do draw the line at techniques that clearly detract from the property's presentation.

The cringe worthy clichés listed above are a good guide of what to avoid.

STAGING DOS AND DON'TS

There are so many aspects to getting your home ready for sale that sometimes it is the simple things that can often be overlooked or not seen as that important. It is important to remember that your house may feel good to you but not necessarily to others, regardless of what your friends tell you. It is essential to appeal to the widest possible cross section of your target market.

Check out my top tips for preparing a home for the market.

1. No house number - this is such a minor detail but so essential! Not only should you make sure you have a house number but it should be in an easily visible location, in good repair and in keeping with the feel of the home. The last thing you want is a buyer's experience of your property starting in frustration because they were unable to locate the property. The same applies for the name of your house, if you have one.

2. Polarising linen - In both the living room and bedroom, the main focal point is the couch or bed. When buyers first walk into these rooms they'll be drawn to those pieces of furniture, so make

sure the linen and accessories (such as cushions and throws) are neutral and mainstream. You don't want them to be boring, but it's important that they don't polarise potential buyers!

3. Too much furniture in each room – It is essential to remember that when a home is open for inspection, in many cases there are multiple parties viewing the property at any one time. Too much furniture will make a room feel smaller than it is.

4. Pet smells – Research tells us that one of the biggest factors that impact negatively on a potential buyer is a pet's smells and mess. Many property owners do work very hard on removing all smells and evidence of their furry friends, however it is difficult to completely eradicate when you are accustomed to the smell on a daily basis. Ideally you need to get a friend who does not own pets to inspect your property and be brutally honest with you about any odours.

5. Heavy window coverings - Leaving heavy window coverings in place can make a room feel dark and cluttered. I often see older homes with multiple heavy drapes that contribute directly to making the room feel small, dark and cold. In these cases they should go, assuming the window condition and outlook permits.

6. Cleanliness - Another HUGE mistake sellers make is assuming buyers can look past the un-swept floors and dirty bathroom. When the mess and dirt is not your own, many buyers find it to be an extreme turn-off.

7. Selling a house with empty rooms – Empty rooms appear smaller and are uninviting to the potential buyer. You do not want to leave anything up to the buyer's imagination. Take control over how your property is viewed and perceived.

8. Decluttering to the point of emptiness – There is a fine line that

runs between a well-staged home and a home that has been decluttered to the point of being empty. Once the line has been crossed the space is no longer inviting and appealing, instead it is cold and vast.

9. Participating in a roadside collection - Roadside collections are a wonderful service and really come in handy when you are cleaning up and preparing your property for sale. However it is essential that the roadside collection period does not overlap in any way with the property going on the market.

10. Take styling to the next level - When people think home staging, they most likely think of throwing a cushion here and there. But to make your home stand out you really have to go the extra mile! So create the finished look by adding details such as homewares, artworks, lighting and rugs. Rugs in particular can be great for tying a space together, especially if your home has an open-plan layout.

www.naomifindlay.com/bookbonus access to periscope videos

DON'T FORGET YOUR OUTSIDE SPACE

My advice so far has been very much focused on the interior living areas of your home.

But another big ticket item on many buyers' agendas is the outdoor space offered by a property.

Whether it's a big backyard for the kids to play in or a stunning entertaining area perfect for hosting that Sunday BBQ, property owners need to ensure they highlight those exterior features that can really help get a sale across the line.

We are very fortunate to live in a warm climate in Australia, so make that count by creating an outdoor space that is a feature of your home.

And don't worry if the space is small, you can still make it luxurious! Ensure it feels like an extension of your indoor space by adding interior pieces such as cushions and throws, combined with nature-themed accents like potted plants.

Property owners also need to ensure they spend time getting their yard in tip top shape. There's no point making the interior spick and span if potential buyers walk outside only to be greeted by long grass and weed-filled gardens.

1. Remove the Debris - Leaves, stray sticks, stones etc. are not appealing. Maintaining a visibly clean yard can make the world of difference.

2. Weed - It's the little things that can make massive differences in your yard appeal. Having a backyard - or front yard - free of weeds makes it look healthier and can show that you really do care about your lawn and garden beds. Weeds can be an

absolute pain to get rid of, but it is an incredibly important step that many people overlook!

3. Your yard is like your hair - If you don't get it trimmed regularly, it soon becomes impossible to tame, and your next haircut might seem like it is way too short! It's important to regularly mow your lawn to make sure the grass is even and looking healthy. Remember to trim around the edges to make sure the ends of your yard don't grow faster than the middle.

4. Keep it hydrated - The grass will become dry and a dull shade of green if it's not watered regularly. Watering the grass might seem trivial - sure. But just think, when it rains there might be some areas that are sheltered from the rain, thus not growing as fast as the areas that do get water. Make sure to water your yard evenly to improve your chances of having a lush lawn for your open home inspections.

5. Plant seasonal plants and flowers - Broad leaf foliage plants are great for year round growth as they can withstand cold and hot temperatures and are very adaptable, but make sure you keep them away from walkways as they can be very sharp. For plants that are suitable for your area and space, make sure you research online (you don't want to plant something that won't grow!) and check out your nearest plant nursery to see what is available both seasonally and locally.

6. Trimming - Trimming back any hedges, trees or large plants can make your house appear more inviting.

7. Make that finishing touch with mulch - Not only will it make your yard easier to maintain during the sale period but it will provide that well finished and cared-for look. Make sure you choose a mulch type that suits the style of the garden

chapter 7

STYLING

"Decorating can be made simple and quick if you work on what you already have. Don't try to re-invent the wheel."

Naomi Findlay PhD

STYLING

When you think about what's involved in preparing your property for sale, I truly believe one of the best analogies you can use to describe the process is baking a cake.

For a cake to be truly amazing, it not only needs to taste amazing, but also feel amazing and look amazing to provide a total experience that leaves you thinking 'wow!'

Preparing your home for sale or valuation can be very similar. The elements we have looked at so far correlate to finding the recipe you want to create, gathering the ingredients and then baking the actual cake; ie conducting your research about other homes for sale, de-cluttering, preparing your property and undertaking maintenance and upgrades.

SO WHERE IS THIS GOING? YOU ASK.

Well now it is time to think about how you are going to ice the cake - that is, how we want the property (cake) to appear when it "goes to market".

The icing or decoration of the cake is effectively the final styling of the property.

But remember - no matter how pretty a cake looks, if it is not baked well it will leave the buyer feeling let down. And conversely, the best baked cake in the world may end up sitting on the shelf way past its use by date if the icing is sloppy or unappealing.

The same can be said when you put a property on the market. The styling cannot "fix" a poorly prepared property, while a poorly styled home will not be "saved" by the fact it was well prepared.

So, having ensured your property preparation is completely up to scratch, it is now essential I arm you with what you need to nail the final styling.

Five steps to styling a space

DEFINE FUNCTION

Before choosing colours, fabrics and finishes, the first essential step when styling your home is deciding on what the space is to be used for - or space planning. When this is done well, the finished product often presents as a larger and more efficient space during your open home inspections.

What you need from your space will greatly depend on your target market - are they parents with young children, a single professional, a married couple?

Assign functions/needs within each space or room in the home, thinking about the size of your furniture and how many people will be in that space at any given time.

Think about what functions should be next to each other to suit the lifestyle of your target market, ie. the dining table next to the kitchen, a play area for the kids next to the kitchen.

Think about the existing shell of your space. Unless you are completely re-modelling, your style makeover will need to work around existing doors, windows, electrics etc.

Think about paths in your space that allow people to move through them easily.

Sketch out your ideas about furniture placement and space planning until you have come up with a plan that works.

DISCOVER YOUR STYLE

Very few people would be certain of their own interior style preferences, let alone be able to describe the style of the property they live in or own.

Discovering your own style can be a fun and eye-opening exercise, but when you are selling it is not all about you.

The most common error I see among properties that have been put on the market is that the property has been presented using items that work against the overall style of the home.

Instead of creating a seamless style that is subtle enough to not look overly "staged" or put on, but striking enough to give your home that wow factor, a poorly styled property filled with mismatched items will jump out at a potential buyer – in all the wrong ways!

Knowing which group your property fits into will guide you through the process of styling the home, allowing you to select the correct furniture and accessories that complement the overall look.

But don't let all those quirky style sub-groups frighten you ie. industrial chic, urban, provincial, romanticism, minimalism etc.

Start instead by discovering what larger decorating group you may belong to. The three most common styles are Traditional, Modern and Fusion (a blended style).

TRADITIONAL

Some home owners don't like using the word "traditional" when they refer to the style of their home, scared that it really means "old", "out-of-date" or "boring".

This is far from the truth. A traditionally styled home is more likely to include strong, classic pieces in warm colours, which help create a feeling of comfort or cosiness.

And traditional styling doesn't have to mean formal either; dark timbers for the floors or large pieces of furniture can be softened with a well-chosen lamp or splash of greenery, while rich colours can be added to provide a luxurious accent to the casual comfyness of that overstuffed armchair or lounge.

Any formal overtones can also be softened in the details, choosing furniture with smooth curves instead of sharp edges, the use of "soft" accessories such as cushions and throws, or adding a touch of wrought iron among feature pieces.

styling

Discover your style

Define your function

Finding your colours

Using your placement

MODERN

Just because a property isn't "old", doesn't mean that it is "modern". This style, also often referred to as a contemporary look, is instead defined by neutral colour schemes (think cool white, stone and grey tones) and smooth clean lines - nothing overly fussy or extravagant, just simple, geometric shapes.

While some people may find it too cold or clinical, this perceived "hard" feeling can be given a lift with bright bursts of colourful accessories - although stick to variants of one or two shades and tones or you risk ending up with a garish rainbow effect.

FUSION

Most homes I see fall into this category - rather than being either traditional or modern, their style is a blend, or fusion, of the two.

Done correctly, this can work particularly well in terms of opening up the property to the widest possible market of buyers - both will pick up on aspects they love, while the understated nature of both styles within the blend will ensure neither ends up as a turn-off.

A fusion style takes the clean lines and pared-down style of the modern look and enhances it with a deftly sprinkled selection of traditional furniture or accessories.

It cuts through what some people may see as the "clutter" of a completely traditional look, while retaining the sense of comfort and warmth often lacking in the strict modern styling.

In doing so, it creates a feeling of homeliness that can allow any buyer to feel a connection to the property, regardless of their own overriding personal tastes.

USING COLOUR

Colour evokes emotions in us all. For example whenever I see dusty pink and sea green together, I'm immediately transported to a beautiful and calm outdoor courtyard.

Colour and colour combinations can be so powerful as to change our mood without us even knowing it.

Many interior designers will agree that colour is the single most important element in interior design and styling.

We all love colour and are naturally drawn to it as human beings, but many of us are afraid to use it so continue to live in neutral white and beige interiors. Don't let colour overwhelm or intimidate you!

Of course, you also need to be careful when styling to sell that your colour choices won't overwhelm or intimidate your potential buyers! Colour choices in this instance are not about your tastes, rather they need to appeal to the widest possible market.

That doesn't just mean white, white and white though! While you may opt for a neutral palette for your base, you can add some extra life to the look by injecting accent colours that create certain feelings into your space.

One way of doing this is to consider the function of the space you are decorating. Is it a study area? Try an accent colour that inspires productiveness rather than relaxation such as shades of oranges and purples. Or are you styling your bedroom? Go for colours that evoke a restful calm such as blue or soft green.

The effects of colour are endless. You can use it to make a room appear larger or smaller, boost energy levels, increase appetite, reduce glare or improve low lighting etc.

Just remember to take it easy - too many colours can end up being confusing for your buyer and leave them wishing for a world of white!

CONSIDER PLACEMENT

The placement of your furniture, artwork, accessories and rugs is vital when creating a well-balanced interior. It's so important to get the balance right in a space (or the right distribution of visual weight). Without balance, there is no harmony.

Is there a focal point in your room? A fireplace, large French windows etc. The placement of your furniture will be guided by this focal point.

Placement of furniture can make a room appear larger. Placing your sofa even just a few inches away from the wall will make the space appear larger.

Consider placement of your window furnishings. Curtains hanging all the way from the ceiling to the floor make the ceilings appear much higher than they actually are.

The wrong placement of furniture can create "dead" space. For example, putting a dresser or small entertainment unit in a corner on a diagonal will create a dead black space behind it. Wherever possible furniture such as sideboards and dressers should be flat up against a wall.

Placement of artwork - people have a tendency to hang artwork far too high on a wall, creating imbalance. Art and mirrors should be hung in relation to the furniture around them.

LIGHTING

Consider placement of lighting in the space. Spread the light sources around the room to create balance.

Again, the function of the space will determine the type of lighting used. Consider whether you need task lighting for reading, sewing, working on the computer. Or is this room purely for relaxation and watching TV, where you may choose to spread some ambient lighting in table and floor lamps.

Create mood with lighting. Lighting can make you feel a certain way, just like colour can. A bright and well lit room can create an up-beat and lively feel. A room illuminated with soft lighting and a few candles will make its occupants feel more intimate and perhaps a little romantic...

Consider decorative lighting - that is, lighting that has no function other than to highlight a feature of the room. For example you could direct a spotlight up under the foliage of a plant, or highlight a beautiful piece of artwork with a downlight positioned appropriately.

THREE MISTAKES TO AVOID WHEN STYLING YOUR HOME!

From the everyday renovators on TV shows to the interior design blogs and magazines, styling and decorating your home no longer looks out of reach. But even with all these great resources, people still make mistakes; after all, not everyone is a trained designer! Here are three errors I often see rookies make and how you can avoid them.

1. Less is more

Accessories and styling items can truly make or break a room, however, these pieces are often given the least amount of attention. People get so carried away with transforming an entire room that when it comes to the crucial stage of styling, the items get thrown together at the last minute. Therefore, the end result can look unnecessarily busy or haphazard and ruin an otherwise well-balanced and inviting space. Make sure you plan those styling items well in advance and give careful thought to what accessories and soft furnishing you actually need. Less can truly be more!

2. Don't be emotionally attached

Everyone can get a bit too emotionally attached to a certain accessory, whether it is an obsession with miniature dolls or a love of the colour yellow. And while giving your room that personal touch is great when you're living there, when you're styling to sell it can potentially end up as a major turn-off for buyers. Channel your professional stylist and detach yourself from all personal effects. Do these decorative pieces actually look good in the space or are they just something you like in isolation?

3. Prioritise function

Often people will use impractical accessories or place their items in a certain way that focuses on the beauty of the room while impeding the room's actual ability to function. This is a big no-no! Function is just as important as visual appeal. If you are using accent items, which are more about aesthetics rather than function, be sure their inclusion isn't disrupting the use of the room. Give the flick to tables in the hall that require you to turn sideways to fit past as well as vases and breakables in a busy thoroughfare of your home.

The three must-haves for every room of the house

While furnishings and accessories like cushions and art are an important aspect of transforming your house into a home, there are three much more important elements: contrast, layers and life. These three must-haves give your home a feeling of interest, depth and texture and make your space enviable, stylish and a place anyone would be delighted to call home!

When looking at styling your home you can achieve amazing results if you focus on some key must-haves in every space. Many of you would now be thinking: colour, cushions and lights! And yes, these things are important, but they are not always translatable from space to space. Take a step back and look at your must-haves from a broader perspective, including contrast, textured layers and life. Putting these into any space of your home will have it looking amazing.

CONTRAST

Regardless of the style, colour preferences or space, contrast is an essential element to be included in all spaces. Contrast can be light and dark or hard and soft. Experiment with small amounts of contrast to start with. Having a great contrast in a space can help define a focal point or a room feature. It is a great way to make sure rooms don't look too uniform or bland.

LAYERS

Layers in a room create interest, texture and depth. This can include layers created with soft furnishings such as rugs, cushions, throws and curtains, or with decor items like art, mirrors and accessories. You can layer by introducing pattern, colour, shape, texture and light into a space. Work by trial and error. Take a photo of what you have done and review the photo a few days later, this will help you edit at a distance and tweak it until it feels right.

LIFE

Signs of life and personality in a space can be the finishing touches that are often missing (or are an after-thought). By life I mean a living plant, flowers, coral or even a piece of your own life, such as a piece of drift wood you collected while camping or a lovely stone you found at the local lake. Bringing life such as plants or organic items into a space, can add life to your home in a way furnishings, accessories and art cannot. These elements can soften corners and add texture and contrast to a space effortlessly.

Incorporating these three must-have elements into each space you style will give you a home that is welcoming and well finished, regardless of its overall style.

The six rules to create a decorative vignette

A vignette is a small decorative arrangement you can stage on any flat surface, from a coffee table, dining table or kitchen island to a fireplace mantel or bookcase.

Wherever you choose to stage your vignette, the decorating principles are the same. Below are six rules to help you create a successful vignette in your home.

1. Use odd numbers

The general rule of a vignette is to group together an odd number of things, usually 3, 5 or 7. This stops your vignette from looking too symmetrical by arranging along half lines. As with any rule, however, there will always be exceptions so don't be afraid to use even numbers of things on occasion if you feel it works.

2. Vary the height of your items

Using items of varying height naturally creates a lovely path for the eye to dance along as it moves from one item to the next. It also means each piece has its own space to shine at each different level rather than competing on the same eye level as the other elements of the vignette.

3. Vary the depth of your items

For the same reasons as above, have the items set at different depths rather than in a row. Encouraging the viewer's eyes to meander through the space will help with the rhythm and balance of the vignette and also motivates people to look at more than one item.

4. Add an unexpected texture

Reward viewers by adding an element with a contrasting texture, for example a piece of found timber or a smooth and shiny metallic element. As the viewer investigates the vignette and pays closer attention to the detail, the contrasting texture will surprise and delight. Adding this touch can add something really special to the vignette, especially if it also has a story.

5. Leave space for the eye to rest

Make sure that there is room for the eye to enjoy and rest on the elements of the vignette by leaving a little space between the focal point of each item. Just like designers use negative space to allow the design to 'breathe', don't have the vignette so packed and busy that it becomes distracting or hard to focus on the different elements. Items in the vignette should work together; you don't want the eye bouncing around it like a ping-pong ball.

6. Inspire yourself

Don't be afraid to look at what other people have done with their vignettes. It's okay to appropriate what you've seen by pairing techniques or ideas with your own items and your own take on something. Check out the monthly Interiors Addict 7 Vignettes competition theinteriorsaddict. com/7vignettes on Instagram or visual networks like Pinterest for great sources of amazing vignettes. You will undoubtedly be very inspired!

How to decorate when you are time poor!

Decorating can be made simple and quick if you work on what you already have. Don't try to re-invent the wheel. Look around, get creative and build on the look you have most likely already started.

Bring the outdoors in for a fresh look. Do you have outdoor stools or an old wrought iron chair sitting outside that are rarely seen or used? Give them a fresh coat of paint in a bold hue and use them indoors to add interest and colour in very little time.

Spruce up your kitchen quickly by checking out the insides of your overhead cupboards If they're display worthy, why not take the doors off and create an open display cabinet with your best crockery or wine glasses. For even greater impact, create a dramatic backdrop by painting the inside of the cupboards in a bright colour, or even cover them with bold wallpaper.

You could also paint your boring old splashback with tile paint in a new and exciting colour.

Rugs, rugs, rugs! Incorporate large and warm floor rugs, particularly to living areas with tiles or floorboards. Not only can this be a real show stopping piece of art, it also anchors the room and gives your space definition.

Add a formal touch to your living area in no time by hanging glamorous drapes over your windows. If you don't have the time or inclination to make the drapes yourself, outsource that time-consuming part or purchase them ready-made. Make them almost ceiling to floor in length to add height and drama to your room.

Bring tired, old furniture to life by giving it a quick coat of paint. This could be an old sideboard, wooden chair or bedside tables.

Accessorise! Never underestimate the impact that a few scatter cushions and throws in complementary colours can make. These items make a room look finished and have the ability to tie everything together.

Replace old lamp shades with new ones to instantly update the lighting in your room.

A quick fix for an old and tired-looking sofa is to purchase a slip cover, giving it a fresh and clean makeover. Slipcovers are getting better and better, with a great range of styles and fabrics to choose from.

And if you're REALLY time poor ... hire an interior decorator or stylist to do all the hard and time consuming work for you!

www.naomifindlay.com/bookbonus access to periscope videos

chapter 8

SPECIFIC TOPICS I COME AGAINST EVERY DAY

"Create a 'view' with your mirror. Place a mirror on the wall opposite a window with a pretty view and voila!"

Naomi Findlay PhD

STYLING A SMALL BALCONY

No matter how high, small or awkwardly-shaped your balcony is, never fear! It's easy to breathe new life into it with these top tips.

Consider how you think buyers would like to use the space. This will determine your choice of furniture. For example, are you wanting to offer an alfresco dining option? Then you will want to invest in a sturdy outdoor dining setting that is in proportion to the space, i.e. ensure there is room to pull out the dining chairs and sit comfortably.

Alternatively you may prefer to create an outdoor space for relaxing with a book and a cuppa. If so, you should be leaning towards an outdoor lounge or armchairs that will see the property's new owner reclining their afternoons away.

Add life and colour to your outdoor space with a container garden. The size and shape of your balcony will determine the possibility of large troughs or smaller pots to create your instant garden. Don't forget to think about how much sun your balcony is exposed to, as it will help determine the placement and choice of your foliage.

Consider your choice of plants carefully as they dry out in pots quite quickly and some need daily attention in the hotter months. Also consider plants that attract butterflies for a fluttery fauna visit every now and again!

If the backdrop to your balcony is a stark rendered or brick wall with no personality, simply cover it with something more interesting and textural, for example, bamboo or other decorative screening. There are some striking and affordable products out there, including wooden screening that resemble laser cut steel panels.

Just because this space is outdoors doesn't mean it can't enjoy some bold artwork to add a punch of personality. A bright and breezy piece of art could do just the trick on a boring wall. Also, if the balcony is very small, consider incorporating a large mirror to instantly double the feeling of space.

With some clever planning, your balcony space can be transformed into a space potential buyers will enjoy and be proud of.

HOW TO CHOOSE A FLOOR RUG - DOES SIZE MATTER?

Whether you are wanting your floor rug to be the hero or the quiet achiever that anchors your room, getting the size of the rug is essential to ensuring overall harmony. Scale and proportion are some of the key elements of interior design, and for good reason. If your area rug is not in proportion to the furniture around it, balance and harmony will not be achieved.

For example, a floor rug in a living room that is only slightly larger than the coffee table will end up looking like a door or bathroom mat.

An area rug should define a space by bringing together the objects around it, so it needs to be large enough to do that. It makes a room appear 'finished'.

In a living space your rug should be large enough that all pieces of furniture comfortably sit around it's perimeter (floating), therefore linking those objects together. Alternatively, and even better, you can go even larger and have at least the front legs of ALL seating hanging over the edge of the rug. By doing this you can create the illusion of more space as the eye is tricked into thinking the rug never ends! However, in a dining room the rug should be large enough that when dining chairs are occupied, all four legs of the chair are still sitting comfortably on top of it.

Measure your seating area before you shop for a rug. Where possible, go for a size that is slightly larger than your seating area, ensuring all furniture can sit comfortably on top of it.

In the bedroom a rug usually runs horizontally along the base of your bed with the bottom legs of the bed sitting on it. The rug should be large enough that you step on it when you emerge from bed in the morning. Again, you want to anchor the bed rather than have a rug that is too small and looks like a bath mat.

A floor area rug is often overlooked and in many cases are far too small for the area of choice. Embrace a floor rug, even over carpet to complete your space.

WILL MIRRORS WORK?

What an amazing invention! Mirrors can do wonders for a space.

You can usefully create illusions with mirrors, making a space appear larger by tricking the eye. Here are some of my top tips for using mirrors.

Place a large mirror on a wall, or mirror a whole wall in a small room, and that wall will simply disappear, making the space double in appearance.

Make a space brighter by strategically placing a mirror in positions that will reflect natural light back into the room.

Create a 'view' with your mirror. Place a mirror on the wall opposite a window with a pretty view and voila! Now you have what looks like two windows on either side of the room, also adding a pleasing touch of balance and symmetry.

Mirrors can be purely decorative of course. Decorate with unique pieces as art.

Define a space with mirror. For example, in a large, plush dressing room/walk-in robe, place mirrors at one end to define the dressing area.

Think outside the box! Mirror entire ceilings in very small spaces such as windowless toilets or laundries and watch the space brighten up when the light is turned on. The ceiling will create the illusion of a skylight.

Mirrors can hide challenging problems in your interior. Do you have pillars? Mirror all four sides and the pillar will all but disappear.

Don't forget that mirrors can be used outdoors as well to make a small garden appear larger and brighter, or increase the size of a small balcony/patio.

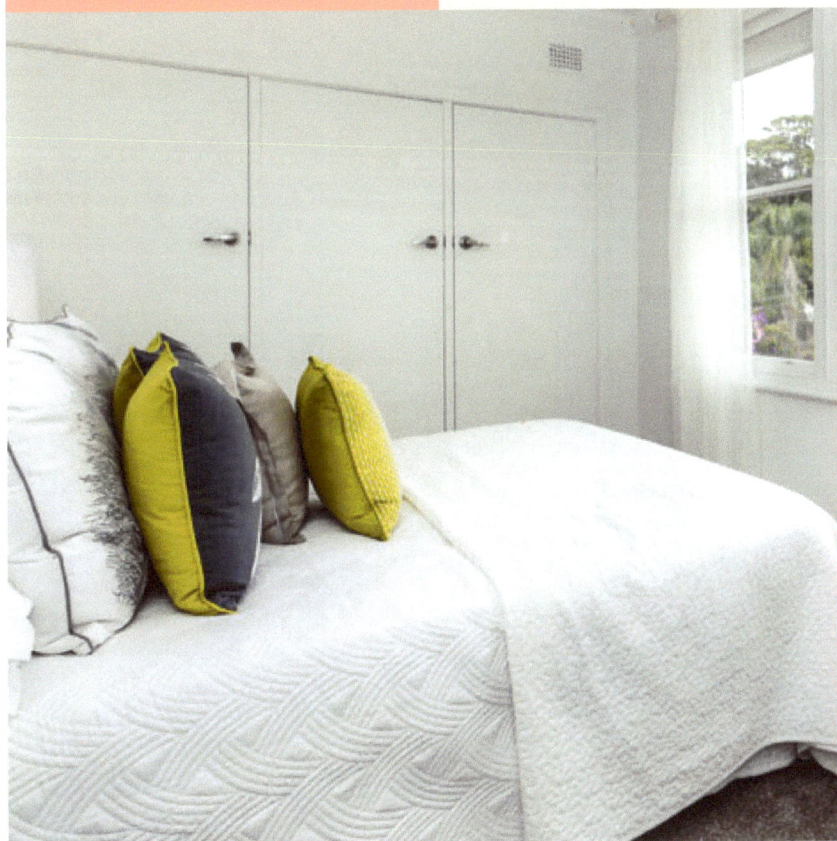

HOW TO ACCESSORISE A BOOKSHELF

There is such a fine line to walk when preparing a property for sale - when people cross the line, the home becomes too impersonal.

On almost a weekly basis I see someone who, in the decluttering process, strips the soul out of the home, emptying bookshelves and peeling them so far back that they are lifeless.

A feast for the visual sense, your bookshelf says a lot about you - and it's not just the tomes that are housed within that do the talking.

The bookshelf presents unique styling opportunities not found anywhere else in the home and you only have to look at Instagram, where the hashtag 'bookshelf' contains more than 270,000 posts, to see that people take their bookshelf styling very seriously indeed.

And, as with all matters of style, what you leave in is as important as what is left out.

DECLUTTER

Like all free surfaces in the home, bookshelves can serve as a dumping ground for domestic detritus. Before you can even think about styling your bookshelf, you should make a serious effort to tidy up your shelves. Whether that means donating a pile of old books to charity or culling an excessive collection of trinkets, this is the first step.

TELLING TALES

A bookshelf provides the perfect space for you to tell people about yourself. Whether it's a couple of beloved knick-knacks from your travels, a statement bauble or a beautiful bunch of fresh flowers, create a series of vignettes on your shelves for added depth and interest.

Photo frames, flowers or greenery, clocks and other ornamental items such as bowls or plates all pack a strong visual punch. There are plenty of fabulous decorative bookends on the market these days - a functional option too. Buy a couple of book stands to display your favourite hardbacks - recipe books are always a good statement piece.

EFFORTLESS STYLE

Ideally, you want a bookshelf that looks artfully and thoughtfully put together - not styled to within an inch of its life. Arrange your books both vertically and horizontally and place a large coffee table book on its side with a decorative item on top for visual interest.

Use a mix of large and small decorative items with a few key pieces to anchor the look - Too many tiny things can make a bookshelf look cluttered. Woven baskets, while also providing extra storage within your bookshelf, inject texture into the space as well.

And lastly, make sure to leave some free space around everything, allowing your books and accessories to breathe.

Colour coding - One for those of the OCD persuasion; the colour coded bookshelf trend took off a few years ago and shows no sign of abating. Playing into our natural desire for order, there's nothing quite as serene as a series of books sorted into their various hues - it also adds a splash of colour with minimal effort and no extra cost. A bridge too far for some, but Zen-like for others, Google it to see what all the fuss is about.

WHAT ABOUT THE WALLS

One thing I have noticed with my clients over the years is that most of them at some stage say to me: "I have this great piece of art but..."

They then proceed to give me one of the following reasons why it is not hung (just to mention a few!):

"I don't know how to hang art";

"I am not sure what height to hang it at";

"I don't know where it goes"; and

"I don't know whether it goes with my other art".

Here are a few pointers to help you be more confident in using the art you have around your home and even creating some yourself.

- Always pick the right height; 99% of my clients hang their art at the wrong height, usually far too high, which means you do not get the chance to admire it as it was intended. The correct height to hang art is at eye level, with the average eye height being approximately 160cm from the ground for an adult. With large pieces, remember to hang the centre of the piece at eye height, not the bottom of it.

- The 'mat board' and frame can have a big effect on the overall appeal of the piece, so before you throw a piece out for charity, thinking it doesn't work in your home, consider what it might be like framed differently. Start by removing it from the frame and taking a fresh look at it.

Use art to accentuate the assets of your room! If you have beautiful tall ceilings, use art to draw your eyes upwards by hanging one piece on top of the other, rather than the more traditional look of side by side.

Don't be afraid to hang images of different shapes, sizes and colours together on a wall. Your pieces don't have to be perfectly matching. When this is the case, use another element to unify the display, such as one of the ideas below:

- Using frames all the same colour.

- Use frames all the same size (but maybe different styles).

- Using frames in the same profile (all landscape, for example).

- There is no need to always have your art hung on walls. Think outside the box and use art at different eye levels within the home, eg. lean a frame on a hall table or sideboard with smaller decorative pieces or books at its base.

- Make sure your art is lit correctly. This doesn't mean you have to install gallery lighting all over your home but be conscious of the lighting around your art. Some art will only shine when light dances onto its surface in the correct way.

Never be afraid to have some fun and experiment with art and images in your home. Art does not have to be all about bright white galleries and expensive pieces, instead it can be all about you and helping you create the style of home you want to spend time in.

FINISHING TOUCHES FOR AN OPEN HOUSE INSPECTION

So you've made it to the final stage of preparing your property for sale: the inspection. Think of the open house as a first date with your prospective buyer: you only get one chance to make a lasting impression.

While it is common knowledge you need to declutter and clean every nook and cranny in the house, do you know the key to making your home stand out during a home open so that it has the best chance to sell for a great price quickly?

It's important to remember that a well-presented home gives buyers the impression that the property is well maintained and therefore, the chances of encountering hidden problems post-sale are minimal.

YOU ARE PERMANENTLY ON SHOW

Although you will not be letting people into your home all day, every day, there is a good chance you will have people driving by to look at the home and assess its street appeal from the minute the property hits the market.

In some cases, this is one way that properties are shortlisted. If a potential home buyer likes photos of your home, they might go ahead and do some research on the street appeal and what other houses in the street are like before they attend an inspection.

There's always the chance you'll need to make a good impression before the buyer contacts an agent, so here are some "housekeeping habits" to get into in order to maximise the likelihood of drive-by buyers wanting to see more:

1. Make sure your front gardens and lawns are well kept and maintained;
2. Remove all junk mail and newspapers from the letterbox and yard as they arrive;
3. Park the cars in the garage, if possible;
4. Avoid having rubbish out for collection on the kerbside; and
5. Each night before sunset, turn on all outdoor lights.

SET THE MOOD

You might not know what the potential home buyer is thinking, but you can do your best to guide them towards positive thoughts by creating a welcoming and comfortable atmosphere in your home.

A great way to set the mood is to think about the senses; what the prospective buyer will experience when inspecting your home.

For instance, open all the windows at least an hour before an inspection to chase away any "house smells". You can also try placing a cinnamon stick in a cup of water in the microwave for two minutes, or plugins, candles and oils to add a subtle fragrance in your house.

To add to the mood you can play some non-offensive music in the background, keeping in mind that everyone has different tastes.

And do remember to adjust room temperature accordingly, making sure that it is comfortable for visitors walking in and out of the house.

ALL TRIMMINGS GREAT AND SMALL

Whether you already accessorise or not, it's the little things that help create a great impression.

"A well–staged property should help you emotionally connect and fall in love with the lifestyle it will offer you."

Naomi Findlay PhD

For example, sprucing up cushion covers, putting your newest towels in the bathroom and clearing your paperwork off your desk (no matter how neat it is) go a long way to creating a favourable and lasting impact of the house and its owners.

Other tips and ideas include:

- Buy fresh flowers or foliage, even if it is simply a centrepiece for the dining or coffee table.
- Straighten and align photographs and art on walls.
- Turn off all electronic devices such as computers and televisions.
- Leave toilet seats down.
- Leave all internal lights and lamps on during inspection, especially bedside lamps and standard lamps.

A home that appears to be a fresh, cared for, low-maintenance property is very attractive to most people, so the day your home goes to market should be the best it has ever looked. Inspection time is the moment to make your home shine and stand out from the competition and where you aim to gain the maximum price in the shortest time period.

www.naomifindlay.com/bookbonus access to periscope videos

chapter 9

FREQUENTLY ASKED QUESTIONS

"A successfully staged home will have the buyers emotionally connecting before they start to consider the home from a functional or structural perspective."

Naomi Findlay PhD

Over my years of helping people sell their homes for more money and sooner, I tend to encounter the same questions time and again from vendors - and even buyers - wanting to know the best way to solve a particular problem, and make the most from their home in the shortest sale period possible.

In this chapter I have included a selection of those most Frequently Asked Questions (FAQ) and the advice I would offer, perfect for people who want to understand the process of preparing and selling their home a little better.

FAQ: What is the best way to advertise my property?

The main methods sellers use to advertise their property are newspaper listings and/or advertisements, online listings and/or advertisements, and leaflet drops. The channel that is best for you is largely driven by the kind of buyer you're looking to attract.

KNOW YOUR BUYER

Selling your property is all about working with a great team, so I asked Mark Kentwell, principal for PRD Nationwide Newcastle and Lake Macquarie, Real Estate Business Australian Regional Principal of the Year 2014 and owner of PRD's Number 1 office nationally, his thoughts on this FAQ.

Mark says there are four main types of buyers you're likely to reach and each have particular behaviours that recommend one advertising channel or another.

1. Active buyers

constantly scour online listings and directly receive alerts from real estate websites and agents. They are highly informed and often conduct a lot of research before they make an offer, which means they are logical and analytical when it comes to purchasing. These are desirable customers who are ready to pounce on a property that suits their needs. Online listings and real estate agent relationships are the best way to reach this bunch.

2. Passive buyers

generally come from the greater local area. They may be active buyers on a bit of a break, or simply happy to see what's out there with no burning desire to buy. The trigger that makes these buyers jump is a match between their aspirations and what your property offers - and this could lead to an emotionally-driven offer. A newspaper advertisement could be the best way to capture a passive buyer's attention.

According to a recent survey from realestate.com.au, 81% of adult newspaper readers read the real estate section even if they are not looking to purchase at that time. If you're going to advertise in a newspaper, keep in mind that the bigger the better. On average, a buyer spends 16 seconds looking at a page and they scan rather than read so use the space wisely to capture their attention and hold them for longer.

3. Neighbourhood buyers

are those who live in the immediate area of a property, and are usually looking to upgrade, purchase an investment, or refer a friend or family member to an area they're familiar with and enjoying living in. You're more likely to find these buyers through a signboard or a letterbox drop.

4. Out of area buyers

will generally do an online search to find your property, so a newspaper ad is unlikely to be the best use of funds to attract these buyers. Invest in communicating details about the proximity of schools, shopping areas, transport and other amenities instead (don't say 'close to transport' when you can say '600 metres from bus stop'). They also love video walkthroughs.

DECIDE ON THE MIX

So we know the four main types of buyers and where they come from, but what you can't predict is where the best buyer(s) will come from. It's important to make sure your campaign has a mix of all channels and the investment is worth the return.

To give an idea of budget, in metropolitan areas a good benchmark is to invest 1% of the property's target value into the marketing campaign and in some prestige or highly competitive areas you might find that 1.5% or so is required to stand out.

In regional areas, 0.5% - 1% of the target value will often do the job of getting you above the competition.

This is separate to the agent's commission, which is the fee you pay for their labour, strategy and skills in running the campaign and negotiating a premium outcome for your sale.

Properties with stand-out marketing campaigns regularly achieve 5% above comparable properties that haven't used a campaign covering all channels. When combined with presentation works and home staging, this can often amount to 10% over the competition, provided the right agent and sale method is used to extract the best from the market.

FAQ: Should I use virtual styling to market my property?

Virtual styling is the practice of using computer modelling to enhance images of a property. You may have seen an artist's impression of a property yet to be built complete with furniture and decor; virtual styling is like that, but uses the actual structure of your home. It can be used to add furniture to empty houses but it also includes any occasion where someone has digitally re-styled its features.

WHAT VIRTUAL STYLING CAN DO?

There are two 'first' impressions that a seller needs to keep in mind when marketing a property. The initial impression is the one used in promotional material such as in advertisements or in online listings: virtual styling is made for driving this 'wow' factor.

If the property is vacant, showing a house with furniture in it will heighten its appeal to buyers; if you have shabby furniture and can't afford to have your property staged in real life, then virtual styling will make a more enticing first impression.

WHAT VIRTUAL STYLING CAN'T DO

The second 'first' impression occurs when a potential buyer visits the property. To sell a property, buyers need to be:

- Attracted to the property.
- Engaged with the property.
- Committed to the property.

Virtual styling will help you *attract* buyers to the property, but it will rarely get them *engaged* or *committed* to the property - that's the role of the inspection.

If the property has been over-enhanced by virtual styling, potential buyers will notice the gap between appearance and reality at the inspection. It's this gap that can curtail engagement and commitment, says Mark Kentwell, principal for PRD Nationwide Newcastle and Lake Macquarie, who believes buyer disappointment on arrival at an opening is impossible to recover.

He adds that the benefit of real staging is that it shows people how to live in the home; for example, a large living space can be used for a lounge/dining/sitting or lounge/sitting/study and if this was un-staged, on inspection they would not be able to see the multi-functional element of the property.

In short, you can make a dump look like a palace with the aid of virtual styling, but you won't be able to sell it on that image alone - you need to pair it with a reasonable level of staging on inspection day to capture the hearts and minds of your buyers.

FAQ: Which is the best season to sell a property?

Think of a real estate 'season' and your mind may immediately fix on spring. The reality is there is no one season to sell a property that will suit everyone. What you need to realise before you focus too heavily on the timing of the sale is that the fundamental driver for property sales is supply and demand.

Mark Kentwell, principal for **PRD** Nationwide Newcastle and Lake Macquarie, says spring has its disadvantages too: competition. If everyone is selling in spring, you're actually part of a glut and that can be bad news if your property isn't especially awe-inspiring.

Waiting an extra month or two can mean the difference between being the shining gem in winter or just one of the pack, surrounded in competition in spring.

TOP TIPS FOR SPRING SELLING

People feel that going on the market in spring will fetch them a better price because gardens tend to look their best, it's the 'nesting' season, and there's more daylight. We're not in London or Vancouver, however - in Australia you can certainly have a beautiful backyard and plenty of sunlight during winter in most areas.

But as a favourite time for vendors to sell, you are likely to be faced with stiff competition. Here's a few tips for the spring selling season.

- Whether it's a lick of paint on your front door or some statement pots either side of it, first impressions really do count. Drag out the high-pressure hose on the driveway to remove oil stains too and trim bushes or hedges in your front garden.

- Declutter - sort methodically through your home, room by room, discarding clutter as you go. Not only will your home look better during the sale period but you will have less to pack away when you are moving out.

- Spring clean. While the light is very beautiful in spring, its brightness can emphasise less-than-clean surfaces. Polish your tapware, remove cobwebs, wash your windows inside and out and dust your blinds. Take the time to polish your floors, mirrors and glass too, as clean reflective surfaces make a space feel larger.

- Repairs and maintenance. Whether it's that tap that has been leaking for the past couple of months or some touch up work that is needed on the paint front, now is the time to get onto repairs and maintenance around your home in anticipation of selling. Fresh paint works minor miracles on tired walls but fight the feature wall urge - neutral colours please most buyers.

- And let's not forget the garden. Remove weeds, mow and edge your lawn and make sure it is kept adequately watered. Plant a few seasonal blooms for a pop of colour and add a sprinkling of fresh mulch to your garden beds for an instant lift.

TIPS TO HELP SECURE A SUMMER SALE

- In case of extreme temperatures, choose your open time carefully - you don't want an open inspection full of people melting.

- As with winter, make sure your property is presented at the optimum temperature by using your air conditioner if you have one. It is important that buyers are comfortable.

- Focus on the highlights of your outdoor spaces by showing people how your property is a great place to spend time during summer.

THE AUTUMN ADVANTAGE

Autumn's mild weather gives you the same advantages of spring without the drawback of the intense competition.

It is a wonderful time to sell, yet sometimes it can be unpredictable weather-wise, so you need to be ready for any situation come open house.

Below are some essential things to remember:

- Make sure there is plenty of light in the space; pull back the heavy curtains and clean the fly screens.

- Make sure that the rooms have additional light sources such as table lamps or desk lamps to spark up the room.

- Be ready for any temperature. Learn to preheat the house and have the air conditioner on until just before the open home. Then turn it down to low (but leave it on) and open the house up (as long as it is not in typhoon season).

- When tending to your lawns don't leave the yards until the day before your open house. If the weather turns bad, you don't want to be put in the situation where you are unable to mow and clean up in time.

- Do all your watering earlier in the week to avoid any dampness come your open house.

- Living in the garden space is a luxury that many people love in autumn, so making outside living an option is a real plus.

- Use transitional styling. Styling your home in winter and summer can be a little different. There are small tweaks that will help you make your home feel open and resort like in summer and warm and welcoming in winter. Make sure that you have both options handy in autumn so you can style to the day of the open house.

ADVICE FOR SELLING IN WINTER

· Choose an inspection time that will maximise daylight.

· For chilly spaces, ensure you pre-heat the property to a comfortable temperature. This is the time to take advantage of that lovely open fire if you have one!

· Consider baking to circulate a pleasant smell and to use the oven to warm up the place. This is the only time when baking is advised.

The only time when it's a bad idea to sell in winter is if the garden is the only highlight of the property.

FOCUS ON DEMAND

According to PRD Nationwide Newcastle and Lake Macquarie data, buyer enquiries vary little more than 10-15% from month to month, season to season; it's the number of properties for sale that can vary quite significantly. Be the seller that makes hay whether the sun is shining or not by hitting the market when supply is low and buyers are still keen to purchase.

FAQ: How do I style my outdoor space?

There is nothing more Australian than inviting friends over for a BBQ, but how do you transform a neglected space into something more appealing when the time to sell your property arrives?

Try these top five tips to create a stylish entertaining space any buyer would love to make their own.

1. Outdoor furniture

Whether you choose lounges or a more traditional table setting, seating is of the utmost importance in this space - you want buyers to feel comfortable with the idea of entertaining there. Gone are the days of the plastic outdoor dining setting - there are plenty of affordable and stylish options to create the ultimate alfresco dining setting.

2. Accessorise

Update your space instantly with a collection of outdoor cushions in on-trend colours and patterns. Outdoor fabrics have come a long way of late, allowing you to beautify your outdoor sofas as you would indoor ones.

From outdoor sculptures to water features and fireplaces, there are no rules when it comes to accessorising outdoors. And the ultimate accessory would have to be a wood-fired pizza oven as it lends an earthy vibe that is pretty tasty too!

3. Plant maintenance

For starters, whip out the weeds and tend to any pressing plant matters by replacing struggling ones with newbies, particularly if you are updating this area in spring. If your thumb is far from green, consider employing a gardener to come in for a one-off overhaul and pre-sale spruce.

One of the hottest trends of the moment - green walls - makes a great outdoor feature, especially when space is tight. They make a small space appear larger and provide a lovely injection of nature into inner-city abodes.

As an aside, property sales data reveals that a properly landscaped abode not only sells more quickly but yields a stronger sale price too.

4. Pots

Think outside the box with this one as there are heaps of options to choose from and a seasonal update can have your garden looking on-trend in no time.

5. Lighting

Just as it works inside, lighting is a great tool for creating ambience and an inviting feel - offering buyers the idea that the area is perfect for entertaining both day and night. Highlight feature plants or pots for nocturnal entertaining – ensure there is adequate lighting around the BBQ and footpaths too.

FAQ: How do I renovate like an investor – with return on investment in mind?

When renovating to sell, objectivity is key. Aim for neutrality over individuality for the greatest return on investment.

Renovating as an investor demands that your personal wants and needs are put aside, with a focus on the bigger picture instead. Where your home may allow you to indulge your every design whim, renovating an investment property demands a considered approach that appeals to the broadest possible target market.

MEET EXPECTATIONS

Make sure you meet the market, and your competition, in regards to expectations for the property. If it's situated in a blue-chip area, it pays to renovate with a more high-end spec as the market demands and expects it. Likewise, if your project is in a cheaper or more affordable locale, be sure not to over-capitalise.

MASS APPEAL

You can never go wrong with white and timeless finishes can easily be made appealing to the individual market with clever styling. Cupboard fronts, bench tops and floors are very expensive to replace - keep them neutral to appeal to the largest subset of buyers. You want people to imagine themselves in the home and a neutral palette allows them to project their own ideas onto the space.

KEY AREAS

When it comes to deciding which rooms to renovate, bathrooms and kitchens are key, as are outdoor living spaces if applicable to the property.

But it is not all about expensive finishes with these spaces, as functionality is just as important. With the popularity of home renovation shows, buyers are a very savvy bunch now and many will immediately notice if a bathroom layout is dysfunctional or inefficient.

With our enviable climate, the outdoors is such an integral part of the modern Australian lifestyle. If there is a way to blend your outdoor space seamlessly with the inside, do it. Think large areas of glazing that take in the outdoors, or bi-fold doors that open onto a deck.

Also, don't forget your property's façade. Most buyers usually make up their mind about a property upon arrival. As such, addressing its street appeal is very important for reeling potential buyers in.

VALUE ADD

It sounds obvious but you must always look at ways of adding the most value when renovating as an investor. If you add value to the property, you are more than likely increasing its sale price too.

While renovating as an investor requires a clear head and tunnel vision, there's nothing quite like the feeling when you come out on top.

FAQ: Should I use a freestanding bath or an inset bath?

I have clients ask me on every bathroom renovation I do, should I really have a freestanding bath? The answer is not a simple one and it is something you need to consider with specific attention to what you want from the bathroom space and the lifestyle it is portraying to potential buyers.

To help make this decision check out my pros and cons below.

WHY FREESTANDING BATH TUBS ARE AMAZING...

- Visual Impact - This one might be arguable, depending on one's personal aesthetic, but freestanding tubs win hands down on most occasions for the striking visual impact they offer!

- They don't require additional framework to be built in, which saves on time and costs, as they also don't require tiling of a hob around them like inset baths.

- Flexibility in placement. The fact that they are finished on all sides means freestanding tubs can be placed anywhere, even in the centre of the bathroom if desired, which can have an amazing impact.

- Negates the need to have a tiled hob around the bath, which minimises grout lines that can then become dirty and need maintenance and cleaning.

- If they become damaged or you want to update it, you rarely have to make structural changes or retile.

THE DRAWBACKS OF THE FREE-STANDING TUB...

* In many cases there is nowhere to store items ie soap, shampoo and conditioner, unless you use a bath caddy or a freestanding stool beside the bath.

* Freestanding baths (especially the amazing stone ones) can be very heavy and might require floor reinforcement or at least a check of the subfloor's strength before installation.

* When placed close to a wall they can be very difficult to clean around, so ideally there would be enough of a gap between the wall and bath to allow you to get in and clean the floor and wall tiles well.

* Some freestanding baths can be quite expensive.

* Freestanding baths can have quite a high side and hence make bathing children or getting in and out more difficult.

All things considered, the decision to go freestanding or an inset hob bath is very dependent on the space you have and the needs of the bathroom space in the property.

FAQ – What to look for when buying a staged home

While my work with clients is on staging a home to sell, they also often ask me what they should look for in a staged home as buyers.

Very simply, a professionally staged home should highlight the positive aspects of the property and minimise the impact of the less impressive.

When I talk about a property's highlights, this can be anything from the open-plan living space, to the view from the deck or the child-friendly backyard and large spacious bedrooms. It's less impressive aspects could include smaller or awkward spaces, tired-looking walls or parts of the property that are not overly appealing to a buyer who is not interested in making any improvements after buying.

Home staging should NEVER conceal, cover or mislead potential buyers. This is such an important point to stress, whether you are staging your own property or having a professional home stager assist you with the process. It is highly unethical to cover or conceal defects or maintenance issues within the home. Home staging is about making the home more appealing, not concealing.

A successfully staged home will have the buyers emotionally connecting before they start to consider the home from a functional or structural perspective. Here are some tips that you can use as a checklist to help you when looking at well-presented or staged homes.

OUTSIDE

The gardens and yards of a well-staged home will be weed free, mulched, pruned and well kept, and rarely present as a yard that requires maintenance. Therefore it is essential that you be realistic about your ability to maintain the yard and gardens. Ask yourself how much time you have and if your thumb is green enough to keep the gardens and yards looking this way long term.

LIGHTING

A well-staged home should always be well lit with multiple layers of lighting. This will include room lighting, task lighting and mood lighting. Be sure that you have a good look at each room and consider how much natural light enters the room, the aspect of the window (eg. north facing) and how much additional lighting is contributing to the space.

FURNITURE SIZE

Room size can be a deal breaker for many people when looking to buy a property. The size of furniture in a room contributes to your perception of how large or small a room is. When considering the size of the rooms in a property be sure to take note of the size and number of furniture pieces in the room. Are the beds full size single, doubles or queens or are they prop beds? Are the lounges two or three-seaters with slim or broad profiles? All of these things will affect our perception of the size of the space.

A well-staged property should help you emotionally connect and fall in love with the lifestyle it will offer you, so it is essential that you use tools to make sure you also consider whether it is suitable for you from a functional perspective!

www.naomifindlay.com/bookbonus
access to periscope videos

naomi's notes

Use the following pages to take notes

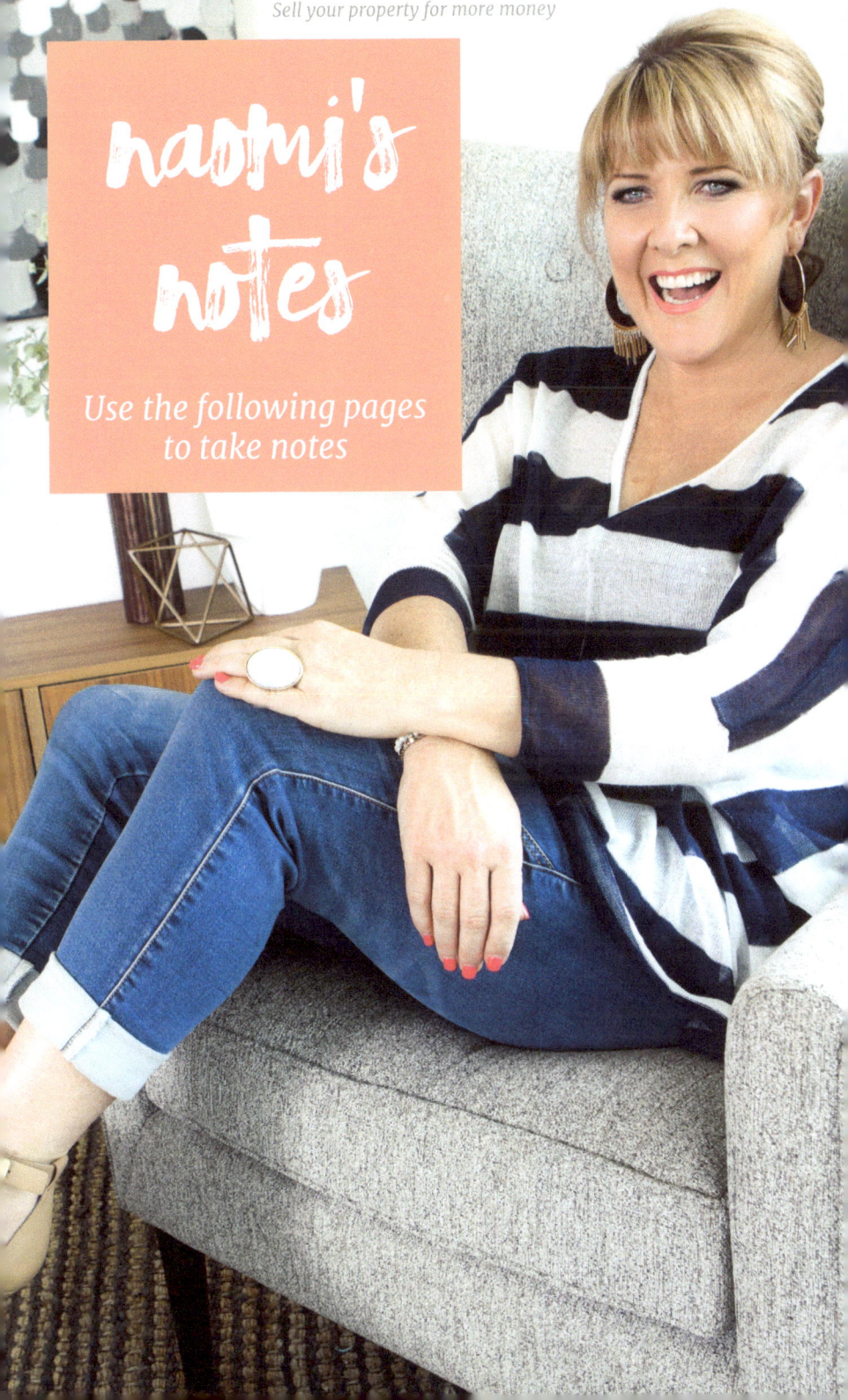

First published by Making Magic Happen Academy, 2017

Copyright © 2017 Naomi Findlay

Cover and interior design by Chantelle Staples

Edited by Teena Raffa-Mulligan.

National Library of Australia Cataloguing-in-Publication.

ISBN: (sc) 978-0-9945265-2-6

ISBN: (e) 978-0-9945265-3-3

Visit the author: www.naomifindlay.com